Many thanks Brian
Valued photographs to which I
am forever grateful.

Best wishes.

Robert C. Turner.

31.3.1990

Black Clouds & White Feathers

Southern Steam from the Footplate

by Robert C. Turner

Illustrations by Brian Morrison & R.C. Riley

Oxford Publishing Co.

Dedication

To my wife Margaret, for her invaluable contribution in assisting me with my researches and my three children, Josephine, Jeremy and Timothy for motivating me to write the book in the first place.

A FOULIS-OPC Railway Book

© 1990 R.C. Turner & Haynes Publishing Group

British Library Cataloguing in Publication Data
Turner, Robert
  Black clouds & white feathers
  1. Southern England. Railway services: British Rail.
  Southern Region. Steam locomotives. Firing, history –
  Biographies
  I. Title
  625.2'61'0924
ISBN 0-86093-457-8

Library of Congress catalog card number
89-85908

Published by:
Haynes Publishing Group
Sparkford, Near Yeovil, Somerset. BA22 7JJ

Haynes Publications Inc.
861 Lawrence Drive, Newbury Park, California 91320, USA.

Printed by: J.H. Haynes & Co. Ltd

Contents

Bricklayers Arms Branch Line

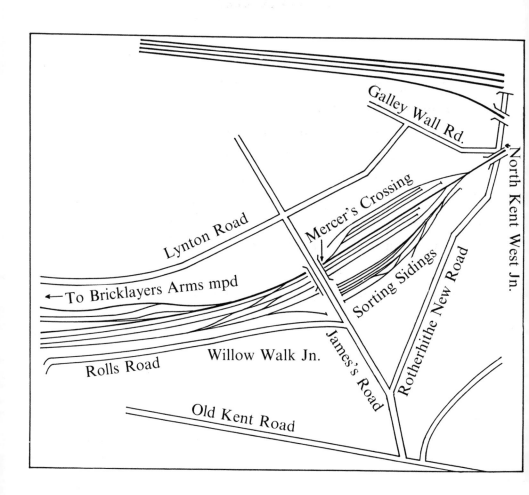

Introduction

The year 1968 was a particularly sad one for the steam enthusiast as the time had come to phase out steam traction for good. For the schoolboy, the dream of becoming a steam engine driver was no longer a prospect, and was confined to the realms of fantasy.

It was just twenty years earlier, in 1948, that the railways in Britain were nationalised. In that very same year, a new and important invention, namely the 'transistor', paved the way for modern technological advancement. This forward step became an early spoke in the wheel of progress, slowly and deliberately turning and making its advancement manifest.

The purpose of this book is to try to turn back the advancing wheel of modern technology and resurrect the arduous times of the steam engine, primarily on the Southern Railway during the 1950s. (The former South Eastern section (SECR) and the London to Brighton line (LBSCR).

To visualise the sea with no waves could well portray Rembrandt without his brush, regardless of which, each compliments the other. Surely then, a portrait of a steam locomotive could not be complete without the embodiment of billowing smoke and discharging steam. Hence, the title of this book, *Black Clouds and White Feathers*.

Black Clouds and White Feathers were not only symbolisms of smoke and steam but both were considered notoriously evil or invitingly sweet, depending of course, on individual taste.

The text will rekindle my own authentic experiences on the footplate and will flavour the "aroma" of smoke and steam, a familiar feature that intoxicated, like opium, the bloodstream of all addicted enginemen. Throughout are detailed educational facets which will illustrate some finer specifications hopefully to stimulate the reader.

Accounts reminiscent of that day will also convey demonstrations of engine workings and how they performed, plus actual footplate journeys through Kent ("the Garden of England"), much renowned for neatly decorated apple orchards and acres of vined hop fields which still formulate much of Kent's characteristic scenery.

Furthermore, a somewhat dramatic account tells why a 'Battle of

Britain' class locomotive crashed in South East London twelve years after World War II with appalling consequences. Specific circumstances will explain formulated lessons subjugating time and unforeseen occurrences.

The decline of the steam engine though, meant much more than the passing of time. It brought with it an end to a picturesque and romantic form of travel. It also extinguished a close-knit community of men whose skill and initiative, coupled with a true sense of responsibility and a genuine devotion to duty, can never ever be replaced by the automated push-button diesels and the electric-powered trains operative today. Nevertheless, the majority of steam men were not opposed to change, in fact, they accepted the advantages as fine and clean, less laborious and a much more comfortable mode of power. Together with agreements on improved conditions and pay, it was a step in the right direction from the steam man's point of view and it has since proved to be so.

Remarkably, steam enthusiasts in Britain, partly under the direction of the Association of Railway Preservation Societies (ARPS) have a marvellous penetration into one of the most elite periods of railway history. As a military victor rides in a triumphal procession, these steam philanthropists have been accumulating untold pleasures, not only for those who recall steam but also to those too young to have known about steam railways. They have a large range of exhibits in their possession with many engines breathing smoke and steam in their full glory. Without exception, these preservationists, are subordinately entrusted with that indelible division of time.

To conclude the book I offer an illustrative choice selection of current railway accomplishments which will explain the quality thereof, a true epitome of railway endeavour.

However, despite the present and long term view, steam locomotives will long be remembered, not only for their uniqueness, but also for their personification of charm and splendour which continue to permeate the hearts of all those who love . . . "Black Clouds and White Feathers".

1
Early Impressions and Bricklayers Arms

My earliest recollection of steam locomotives was in North Yorkshire. As a mere six year old boy my brain lacked sufficient knowledge to fully understand the predicament I was in. Britain was at war, or so they said, and I was just one of thousands of confused evacuees commandeered to escape the London 'Blitz', whatever that was!

I was a shy, nervous lad, due perhaps to the forced situation in which I found myself. Nevertheless, I knew I had a mother, a father, three brothers and a sister, and here I was, perplexed, coyly licking away my tears, and standing rigid with Mrs Townsend, a complete stranger (now my guardian). My childish and fragmented dilemma left my imagination somewhat confused, yet the sight and smell of those immense steam engines standing formidably in Harrogate station was to remain a lasting impression in my mind, even more than the sight and smell of home-baked bread and Yorkshire pudding that Mrs Townsend used to make, evoking expressions of: "Eee by gum tha' wer' champion", from the lips of Mr Townsend.

My next close encounter with steam engines was not to be until five years later, just three years after the war. Back in London and understanding a bit more about my whereabouts and the reasons thereof, I discovered I was now the eldest of nine children! It seemed, that World War II had no real effect in dissuading the human posterity process, at least not in my family.

The somewhat dilapidated house in which we lived, with gas and outside closet, backed onto the main London to Brighton railway (ex-LBSCR) between Honor Oak Park and Forest Hill stations in South East London. At the bottom of the long garden and almost hidden by green creeper, was a wire mesh fence which served to protect the railway property from lads like me. Unfortunately, the railway traffic was not directly visible from the fence, for wild growth and a descending embankment obscured the line. Realising the apparent danger, my mother discouraged our venturing beyond the boundary. Her 'finger-waving remarks' categorically emphasised her verbal dictum, "Don't yer dare get-over that fence . . . otherwise a 'Bogie-man' will get 'old of yer".

One early morning at the crack of dawn, I stirred from slumber to a distant rumble coming from over the fence. With one leg out of the bed, my naked limb dangled and my foot touched the cold lino.

"Move up will yer", I snorted to my brother Chas (Charles) who was lying in my place.

"Yerv' got all the bed yoo 'ave."

"It's not me", he shouted in retaliation.

"It's the twins (John and Billy) they keep pushing me over."

"If yer don't move over, I'll hit yer."

Billy slept on, probably dreaming about the girls he knew at school. As he moved over, John pulled the blankets with him.

"Can yer 'ere that Chas?" I said, propping one hand under my chin.

"Can I 'ere *what*?" he grumbled annoyingly.

"That!"

"I can't 'ere anything – only the birds whistlin'", Chas grumbled half asleep.

Falling out of bed, I found that gravity had a stronger pull than the blankets I surrendered to the boys. Creeping downstairs in the half-dark, my thoughts conjured up ideas of the 'Bogie-man'; the scullery door made a squeak which startled me half to death. Returning quickly, I glanced fearfully up the steep garden to where the noise was coming from. Everything was as quiet as the copper chrysanthemums standing near the tall weeds. All that was moving was a faint smoke cloud whispering under a cloudy sky. A far off whistle fractured the dawn somewhat eerily coming in the direction of Forest Hill station. Climbing back into bed, my nostrils itched and I sneezed a wet spray into the back of Chas's head.

"Oi!, yer rotten thing", he said, wiping his neck with the blankets.

Many weeks later, filled with a feeling of defiance and intrepidation, Chas and I launched into the deep unknown beyond the boundary fence. Cautiously we crouched listening in the tall grass and wild bushes. Suddenly it happened! The stilled air was disrupted by a thundering noise which grew nearer and louder. Some sparrows flew off a nearby tree, 'what could it be?' I thought. The rumble was strengthened by bursts of smoke and sparks flying skywards descending to our place of refuge. If only we could escape to the safety of the fence, but it was far too late for that. The er . . . whatever it was . . . was sure to see us. With our eyes wide and our hearts pounding, we saw a black monster appear from obscurity. 'What a relief!' I thought. It wasn't the 'Bogie-man' after all. When I sighted the noisy creature it produced a recollection of the powerful engines I had first clapped eyes on five years earlier in Harrogate station.

The steam engine moved very slowly, not only because of the upward gradient, but it was pulling truck after truck laden high with coal. The yanking of couplings and the rumbling of wheels was overawed by yet a second engine 'pushing' the same trucks and equally coughing out black smoke and cinders. Like the first engine, we saw two men inside the cab, each one wearing a shiny cap.

Emerging from our place of security, we waved nervously. Our confidence was somewhat regained when the crewmen, much to our surprise, waved in return acknowledging our keen interest. Needless to say, that was not my last trespass on railway property!

Eight years later, the tables were turned, for I became a crewman, complete with shiny cap, working yet another coal train 'up' the so-called Forest Hill Bank, destined for Waddon Marsh Power Station near Croydon in Surrey.

I began my railway career, after leaving school in 1953, well before the physical characteristics of modern technology took control. Although fundamentally conceived, the advent seemed far off from my point of view, as a child would reflect on old age.

Bricklayers Arms depot in South East London was commonly known as "B. Arms", or "The Brick" as some older hands preferred to call it. It provided a perfect setting for my first 'real' encounters with steam locomotives. The main 'Swan Gate' entrance was a quick 20 minutes' walk to the world-famous Tower Bridge and situated near the renowned Old Kent Road.

Bricklayers Arms enjoyed a rather lavish and comprehensive range of vehicles which dealt mostly with freight of both road and rail. Inside the main entrance a conspicuously wide esplanade exposed a concerted flow of British Railways' trucks ebbing and flowing in bee-like fashion, loading and unloading varieties of goods. This scrupulous practice caused concern for one's personal safety, for there were no apparent walkways for motive power staff.

The practical design of the railway lorries offered greater manoeuvrability with their single front wheel, and I am sure proved an asset to drivers with their deliveries when driving round confined roads existing in some suburban districts.

Located protectively amidst the extensive goods yards were the motive power sheds (see diagram). The large rail sidings stretched for at least two miles from the main entrance to Rotherhithe New Road, finally merging into a brick viaduct at Corbetts Lane. This two mile range comprised a federation of trucks and branch sidings, that were centralised by two main running lines, one 'up' and one 'down', imitating a long tree trunk culminating its roots in the engine depot.

At North Kent West Junction, near Rotherhithe New Road, the railway junctured obtusely to merge with the 'Old Brighton' section, the LBSCR. Further on, and passing the Rotherhithe Road carriage sidings, a steep ascent married into the South Eastern & Chatham, the SECR. Both these sections still form the existing Eastern section of the Southern Region.

In the early 1950s however, the scars of war were very evident in large degrees. For it was only a few years earlier that Germany began launching the V1 flying bombs in June 1944. Eight thousand of those horrendous "Doodlebugs" were targeted at England, a total of 2,300 of which reached the Capital. The V2 rocket was much larger and faster and quickly followed in the true sense of the word. Because of its tremendous speed, it was neither seen nor heard. The first one crashed in West London in September 1944. These so-called "secret weapons" from the Hitler camp wrought untold havoc, and a great toll of both property and human life was dissected beyond return.

Inevitably many railway stations, railway bridges and sidings were destroyed, hindering railway operations. One such V1 rocket hit the bridge which carried railway traffic over the River Thames to and from Charing Cross terminus. Large parts of the bridge fell into the Thames and steel lines hung like limp spaghetti. Of course, other conventional bombs had their effect too, creating a 'Blitz' of destruction that London had never experienced before.

Although seriously damaged, Bricklayers Arms escaped complete destruction. For myself, as a new and raw engine cleaner, everything appeared normal. After all, what else could a young boy of 15 be interested in, but the pride and the passion of the steam Leviathan.

Suppose we don our overalls and shiny cap and take up a typical day's work in the depot. We will assume that we are on the footplate of a 'Schools' class locomotive which has just returned to the depot after completing a Hastings trip. The experience will follow a sequence of events which will ascertain the fundamental workings of the depot, plus varied subsidiary information that will portray arbitrary responsibilities, flavoured with a safety element. Our driver on this occasion, is my old mate Jack Leigh with whom I worked several times in my early days as 'passed cleaner'. Jack however, was nearing retirement and therefore confined to shed duties only.

There we were, comfortably drinking tea in the crewmans' lobby when a voice penetrated our ears. "Jack, . . . will you and yer mate go and relieve St Leonards' men on the coal-stage?" The familiar voice belonged to Jim Foote, one of the three Running Foremen employed at Bricklayers Arms. Without hesitation, our legs sprung to life and followed the foreman out of the door. We marched noisily on the bare floorboards, spilling tea as we stomped regimentally in the wake of Foote's footsteps.

Boarding the footplate, the St Leonards' men seemed eager to be off, to go and eat their well-deserved sandwiches. The engine stood just inside the Dunton Road Bridge which served as a convenient perimeter to the loco sheds, separating it from the goods sidings on the other side. Close to the bridge, and immediately right on entry, a small cabin accommodated an ex-driver. He was mainly responsible for recording the arrivals and departures of all engines and then furnish the same information by telephone to the running foreman. Most depots provided light duties for men with physical infirmities which disallowed main line activities; such was the case here.

The eye-catching observation from the footplate, and right of the coal-stage on the inlet road, offered a splendid confrontation, an invincible host of live engines noisily expressing their presence. A continuous haze of black and white cloud lifted from chimney and safety valve in turn, obscuring the skyline flirting above the adjacent sidings to slowly filter across the Old Kent Road. This was the 'Old' shed that composed eight roads, four terminals and four roads marrying into the out-of-sight turntable. The triple vexation of smoke, steam and oil, inundated the blood stream pulsating magnetic impulses of coercion, an indefinable aroma, which seemingly, was atrocious to any visitor, but was as sweet as honey to every crewman, figuratively speaking of course.

Creating a fresh vacuum in the brake system, Driver Leigh opened and closed the regulator handle in quick succession to idle the few yards more for coal replenishment. It was vital to stop the 'Schools' in such a way as to allow the coal to fall as near to the front end of the tender as possible for easy reach when firing. Whilst Jack moved the engine I took the opportunity to rake the fire over the fire-grate and closed off both dampers to languish energy to facilitate cleaning the fire.

The baffle-plate or deflector-plate as some preferred to call it had also to be removed. This was a simple device which rested under its own weight and slotted neatly inside the fire-hole door. The blade of the firing shovel was the only effective implement capable of extracting the hot and heavy brute. So I placed the shovel blade firmly under the plate, a firm and sudden lift and pull simultaneously removed it easily, like a cumbersome steel tooth pulled in dentist fashion. Its main objective was supposed to reduce smoke emission, considered a serious offence, more especially in the early days of steam when the baffle-plate was first introduced in 1858 for that purpose. But I found it more effective for its other purpose of protecting boiler tubes against cold air being dragged in when the fire doors were open. It was very helpful too, particularly when working under stress, to direct secondary air on top of the fire to assist combustion, especially if having problems inducing primary air up through the dampers.

Having now removed the baffle-plate, a larger proximity inside the firebox made easier visual contact to inspect boiler tubes, firebox stays, fusible plugs, and the brick-arch. Examination of the aforesaid was most essential for continued efficiency. Generally speaking, it was the driver's job to inspect those vital elements to ensure reasonable condition. Often, tubes became consolidated with sulphate, a harmful compound extracted from sulphur. On occasion, water seepage around tube and stay joints were tell-tale signs of possible fracture, probably due to uneven expansion and retraction by scale build-up, but more about that in chapter two.

The fuse-plugs, or lead-plugs, as they were often called, also required close scrutiny. Both plugs were fitted to the crown of the firebox as a safety precaution against a low water content. If for example, the water level in the boiler fell below gauge glass level, inevitably, the soft lead would melt and jettison steam directly onto the fire. The unfortunate fireman would then have to remove the fire as quickly as possible to save further damage to the tubes and other vulnerable parts.

The brick-arch was another component scrupulously examined. Over a period of time, molten ash lifted from the fire to form incandescent stalactites. Bricks became dislodged and fell into the fire to melt between the fire-bars which had an adverse effect on combustion if not removed. If conditions were not wholly satisfied, the driver shifted the responsibility onto the Running Foreman's

14

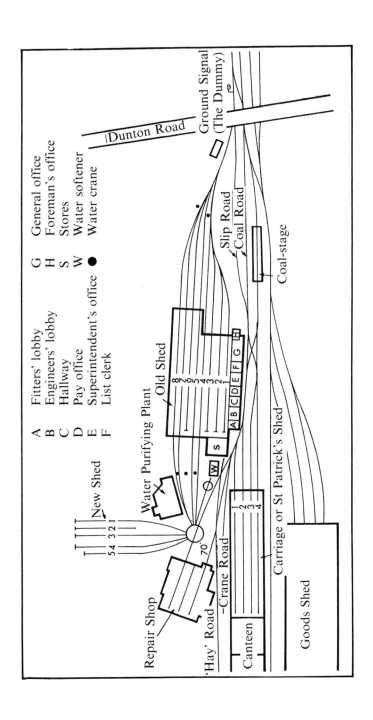

A Fitters' lobby
B Engineers' lobby
C Hallway
D Pay office
E Superintendent's office
F List clerk

G General office
H Foreman's office
S Stores
W Water softener
● Water crane

New Shed
5 4 3 2 1

Water Purifying Plant
Old Shed

8
7
6
5
4
3
2
1

A B C D E F G

S

W

Repair Shop

70

'Hay' Road
Crane Road

Canteen
1
2
3
4

Carriage or St Patrick's Shed

Goods Shed

Dunton Road

Ground Signal
(The Dummy)

Slip Road
Coal Road

Coal-stage

Bricklayers Arms M.P.D.

shoulders, who would then enforce mandatory powers to put the engine right. Common sense and good judgement were no doubt key factors in ascertaining correct decisions, and thus always prevailed.

However, the coaling area was a rather dismal and exposed environment and must have contributed heavily to grime in the vicinity. On wild windswept nights, the draughty and somewhat nauseating conditions were uncomfortable for the hard-working coalmen. The bitter elements must have created a tantalising flavour to say the least. A seemingly favourable advantage was one or two brightly lit coal braziers that offered a small psychological comfort to their onerous task.

During the first century of railway operations, engine sheds achieved a very high standard of cleanliness but, from the Second World War, this enviable reputation deteriorated rapidly. Therefore, engine sheds all over Britain became grime areas, and the Bricklayers Arms was certainly no exception. Most enginemen attempted to minimise the fumes as best as they could, but it was impossible to abate it completely, especially when lighting up dead locomotives. The smoke was beyond control until the engine itself made sufficient steam.

The coal-stage was simply arranged at ground level. One side comprised several 16 or 20 ton trucks which ran parallel to the stage road. The wagons were laden full of black fossil fuel direct from the Welsh Valley coal mines. More than likely, a soft variety, a usual diet of poor and medium grades, a choice of 'just as it comes' was the order of the day and every day. The thick clinker and white ash produced on the fire bed, quite definitely indicated that the poor grade was more available than the latter. As veteran drivers explained, the quality coal was much improved since the war years, but that was no real comfort when sweating blood during the process of removing heaps of solid clinker.

The soft coal provided for steam engines was very slow burning and demanded extreme skill to control a balanced combustion; the reason being that it was low in volatile matter, and so required a large and invigorated fire to outweigh reluctancy. Years of practical experience of course, was the best teacher, which in principle, included the 'little but often' motto that became the rule rather than the exception.

A fireman brought up on soft coal found no adverse effects when firing with Yorkshire Hards; unlike Stewarts Lane and Nine Elms depots, Bricklayers Arms was rarely supplied with hard coal. Engines visited each others' depots for coal top-up and the like, so tenders acquired a mixture of both commodities and no doubt some firemen, perhaps from Stewarts Lane or Nine Elms, having little experience handling soft coal, could encounter firing difficulties. Lessons of combustion control will be discussed later in chapter four.

Standing in front of the large 20 ton trucks positioned on the coal-stage were smaller one ton containers which ran on a narrow gauge track. The coal labourers shovelled the coal by hand from the larger wagon into the smaller steel skip. The fuel controllers was then able to calculate exactly how much each locomotive received and recorded same. Before unloading commenced on any individual coal truck, it was common practice for one coalman to clout two gravity held pins which secured the side door, and a coalpick was readily available for that purpose. It was a dangerous operation, but there were no other means of safer release. When the pins were forcibly disengaged, the dead weight of coal cascaded out and created an avalanche of fuel and dust, an irritable dilemma for the lungs of the coal workers, although some wore mouth protectors. The labourers who opened the side door, could not afford to procrastinate, so a 'Roger Bannister' type reverse sprint was more than ideal to avoid a long stay in the local Guys Hospital, or maybe a permanent plot in the nearest cemetery.

When the smaller one ton skip was full it was pushed manually to the elevator and locked into position. The hoist operator then checked the hopper-like chute situated above the hoist to ensure the special hinged plate was positioned to guide the coal at a 45° angle which subsequently shot the coal into the engine's tender. However, a discreet operator selected the desired position well before each engine reached the electric elevator, according to whether the locomotive was tender first or otherwise. A press of a button activated the motor with a sudden jolt, lifting the laden truck skyward and henceforth tipped its load into the tender, and at the same time blanketing the immediate area with clouds of black filth. Although water sprinklers were provided above the hoist they were rarely used, probably due to neglect, damage or both. Therefore, a brave fireman stayed on the footplate in an attempt to quell the disgusting intrusion. The engine water hose, turned on at low pressure, served the purpose well and prevented the majority of dust penetrating the footplate, but one could never control the muck completely. One real danger when working the engine hose for this purpose, was that one could unwittingly spray the coal labourers. If this happened, the coalman's own specialised vocabulary actuated every adjective not found in the Concise Oxford dictionary, and the somewhat acute articulation embarrassed the black cloud that one was anxious to dispel.

Ensuring an acceptable load, a recharge of perhaps two to four tons was an ample complement for the next trip, unless the running foreman intervened for some other reason. Having filled with coal I systematically secured larger lumps that hung precariously over the tender before Jack moved the engine to our next point of call.

It was always an inviolable rule before moving any loco to blast the whistle as a warning of movement, as there were no static or set signals to observe in the depot, the running was free for all, so discretion, stringent care and attention was adopted at all times, with the emphasis on all three. This practice became extremely methodical for it produced a recognised standard in cooperation and courtesy which exposed a paramount latitude of safety among all concerned. A pity the same conformities are not maintained on the roads of Britain today.

Another habitual pull on the whistle, a yank at the regulator handle and Jack extended our slow venture the few yards to the office. The office was conveniently built-in and located on one corner of Old Shed and integral with it. Its two sash windows offered a superb view of all comings and goings, an important vantage point in more ways than one.

Observing our presence, and providing the weather was tastefully good, the foreman usually met the loco before we stopped to hand paper instructions for the crew. Reaching down from the moving footplate I grabbed the paper informant. At first glance the note appeared as a secret message in code, except it was not exactly secret. The minimal abbreviated scribble was readily interpreted for 'disposing' and 'preparing' the engine for its next duty. The interpretations of the abbreviations will be explained in chapter two.

Looking ahead it was all clear to pass the running foreman's office. The two-way single road now took a slight right curvature to the turntable which also passed the administration block to our right. It was here that enginemen's blue time sheets were converted to green money and distributed every Friday, the pay-day for enginemen.

Crewmen coming on duty had to sign and report their arrival, perhaps long before their official booking-on time so as to ensure that their engine was satisfactorily prepared for whatever journey it had to make. Noticeably too, most crewmen carried either a shoulder bag or small suitcase which contained the sandwiches. But more importantly, the bag also accommodated a tea-can with ready made 'goo', in other words, a mixture of tea, sugar and condensed milk all neatly wrapped in greaseproof paper. The clever idea was, to dip the paper and contents inside the can and then fill with boiling water, a few seconds later, remove the paper, and Hey Presto! . . . a perfect cup of hot tea.

Adjoining the offices, a long corridor displayed notice boards which flanked one side with subservient information. For example the largish glass cases displayed things like: Duty Rosters and Permanent Way Precautions – locations of current repair works and diversions, which more often than not enforced speed restrictions and the like. Furthermore, all drivers were personally issued with these written documents on a weekly basis. For, depending on individual assignments, many duties did not originate and return to the home depot, hence, the notice issue. Moreover, ignorance of printed and posted rules, regulations and subsequent amendments could not therefore be pleaded. It was the prime responsibility of all crewmen, particularly the driver, to miss nothing that was relevant to his duties for the immediate safety of everyone concerned.

Predominantly adjacent to the administration buildings, were the indisputable crew mess-rooms, or 'lobby' as most preferred. A large kettle pre-eminently occupied a gas stove taking up permanent residence and kept on the boil for obvious reasons. Anyone not re-filling the water monster after their use, had to face the wrath of Jack Leigh or George Seal, two drivers retired to shed duties. Incidentally, both these gentlemen drivers also kept the mess-room comfortable and clean, two respected drivers who were loved by all.

The slow pace of the 'Schools' now continued unceremoniously past Mr Boarers' first floor office – the shed controller and master. He was the nucleus of motive power control, the man who was responsible for all constitutional developments in the arms of the 'Brick'. He was also the man who sacked my younger brother for moving an engine without authority and for cutting through a high-pressure hose while the boiler washer was using it, and soaking him like a drowned rat.

A little farther on, a conglomeration of railway clothing now presented itself as we clanked slowly by the stores, the place where protective clothing was acquired and issued annually to railway staff. A wide selection of overalls, serge jackets and railway macs, not forgetting the unmistakable guise of shiny caps, were the usual 'off the peg' productions which put the customary 'fifty-bob tailors' down the Old Kent Road to shame.

Immediately left and opposite the sand-drying shed, was the carriage shed (or St Patrick's Shed) that often evoked a somewhat melancholy atmosphere. The shed adopted a congregation of 'dead' engines (no smoke and steam), a sour picture of depravity and abandonment waiting their turn for tube blowing, boiler washing, repairs and servicing.

Our keen vigil on passing the carriage shed now observed the distinctive 70ft turntable which was invariably set for the approach road. But one could never postulate, for on odd occasions a fireman or driver may have forgotten to return the 'table' to its rightful position. "Whoa Jack!" was my warning cry. Immediately, Jack dropped the handle (apply the brake) and the 'Schools' shuddered to an instant stop. Approaching from the turntable, was a Standard Tank, which sighting our presence, stopped suddenly too. In this position, due to the road layout, it was far easier for Jack to drop back and then forward into the adjacent carriage shed to allow the Standard through. I therefore hopped off the footplate to pull the necessary points. Having completed the shunt, we once again navigated the table approach.

Opposing the turntable was an interesting establishment in the shape of the repair shop, an operating theatre for locomotives where some minor and fewer major operations were performed. The shop stood independently, an impregnable building, for only one road served it from off the table. A large internal overhead crane was sometimes seen lifting the largest of engines with meticulous precision. Every engine, after perhaps 20,000 miles and more working, was subjected to an operational service and thorough inspection of all fast-wearing parts. However, the shop had various facilities for regular examinations and repair, but if the inspection revealed more serious faults or deterioration, the engine was then banished to Ashford Works in Kent where facilities were more extensive. The accompanying photographs show the 1986 derelict condition of the former shop and turntable pit. A sad end to many years of active service, Bricklayers Arms having closed its doors in 1962.

Facing the repair shop was an impresario dwelling considered to be the most important venue at B. Arms, from the staff's point of view anyway – the large 'Canteen'. As always, the menu offered refreshments ideally satisfying for local railway personnel of both road and rail. Inside the large dining concourse, and positioned one side of the floor space, was an array of full-sized snooker tables which dominated the scene. Above the rabble of male voices, deliberating their why's and whatfors, an incense of smoke and steam of a different sort, a small similarity perhaps of 'Old Shed' collaborated persistently, enveloping the high ceiling space. The rich protein intake and crusty bread, supplied the source of influence, which when consumed, re-charged energies for re-newed manpower. One or two visits to the human disposal conveniences were conducive for prolonged and efficient progress. One favourite delicacy I readily devoured (a tradition no doubt adopted from the insidious war years and food rationing) was hot toast, lavishly spread with beef dripping which lubricated the internal combustion chamber adjacent to the human diaphragm, as well as other vital parts.

Back with Jack on the turntable. After securing the engine, we both climbed off the footplate to push the hand-operated paraphernalia round to road four. Depending how full the water tender was, it was often found necessary to re-position a larger loco to obtain an equal balance. Once balance was established, the table's own equilibrium reduced the human effort. It was therefore customary to halt the table for the desired road by using the footbrake, then a steel signal type lever bolted the contraption into position.

Another shriek on the whistle and Jack allowed me to move the engine off to obtain water a few yards on, whilst he returned the table to the approach road. Water however, was considered the most important commodity of all. Every tender and tank engine took advantage at every opportunity practicable, particularly in deteriorating weather conditions or expected and unexpected delays, which could be detrimental to the water supply to make absolutely sure of a maximised fill. At Bricklayers Arms, as it was in every engine depot, it was an automatic procedure, a religious worship, that water top-up was exercised.

There were water facilities on each road of Old Shed, and to every vertical column adhered a rubber hose. At full pressure, a 'Schools' class tender was full in a few minutes. Despite a wide variety of water supplies for steam engines, impurities therein had adverse effects on boiler conditions. Both acidity and alkalinity were recognised as impure elements, the former corroded metal and the latter deposited scale on metal and because of this problem, periodically and according to working miles, most passenger engines were 'blown down'. This practice discharged effluent which had built-up inside the boiler. For this reason, a special valve located on the front under-side of the engine was opened. Of course, both injectors were usually operated to replace the sudden surge of steam and water being imminently lost. Although the operation only took two or three minutes this was sufficient to envelope the complete locomotive in a cloud of steam. The operation, as I clearly recall, became a subject of controversy, for it was theorised that the sudden reduction of steam pressure subjected the boiler to incalculable stress which weakened the boiler structure. But like all theories, careful testing by the experts, is the only way to provide evidence on the matter. As far as I was aware, it remained normal procedure until the end of steam traction on BR.

Our next exercise, after supplementing the boiler and filling the tender with water, was to move the 'Schools' another few yards on, over the ashpit, to carry out the intimate task of cleaning the fire, smokebox and ashpan, and for Jack to lubricate all required parts.

First though, to elucidate safety, we destroyed the vacuum brake (disengage its use), opened the cylinder cocks, left the reversing lever in mid-gear, and finally, screwed the handbrake firmly down. Before we commenced these necessary chores, Jack and I supplemented our own human frames with a slice of hot toast and dripping, washed neatly down with our own special 'goo' of hot tea.

2
Steam Welfare v Chemical Warfare

Nothing makes cleaning and preparing an engine more desirable than to reflect on the horrors of a "Rough Trip". Rough trips were when enginemen had severe difficulties maintaining an adequate supply of steam and water in the boiler which called for extreme effort to keep the train moving. Of course there were many contributory factors for the steam shortage, but this chapter will only highlight the bone of contention behind the scenes; that, apart from a few cuts and bruises, a running battle exalted steam as 'reigning champion'.

The Motive Power Department at Bricklayers Arms, like most larger depots that could afford it, employed provisions to keep the 'iron maidens' systematically clean; in addition, to control or cure potentially damaging engine attacks, which was a never-ending contest in the fight to fortify the nutritive value of steam production.

Like all known power, there must be a first cause; motive power therefore suggests movement by influence. A horse for example; that is the four-legged variety, derives its power from the chemical energy stored in the vegetation it eats. Vegetation therefore is the source of its muscle power. It then disposes of waste products as you know; to continue its strength and proficiency. In similar manner, the source of power to the iron horse is the fuel it consumes which provides the required energy for continued working. Combustion therefore generates the steam, the power and influence which motivates the action. Thus, the 'Iron Horse', like our animal friend, also necessitates refreshment and mucking out too, to further energise efficiency to the highest degree. For these reasons I will now compose some daily and other periodical assaults in the field of steam welfare which became a defensive campaign to execute and destroy the enemy.

The very conditions of a steam locomotive were indeed pleasant when flavoured with respect and consideration. Unsuspectingly at times, a steam engine suffered serious setbacks when not correctly diagnosed. Particularly as far as cleaning boilers was concerned. Very often, despite the good intentions of those responsible, other somewhat acute chemical reactions generated uncomfortable ailments, unwittingly caused perhaps, by administrative ignorance, or just simple neglect.

Scale was a boiler's worst enemy, the undesired concretion deposited inside the tube surfaces attacking and corroding all heating properties.

Interestingly, drinking water can seldom be called pure or clean in a chemical sense, since it almost always contains some gases and minerals dissolved in it. Making water potable or safe to drink does not necessarily require removal of all impurities. In fact; some of the elements necessary to good health and taste are often found quite naturally in good drinking water. Moreover, dissolved oxygen is vital in an amazing step-by-step digestion process which occurs in both moving and still waters neutralizing them, or supporting bacteria that breaks down to a harmless residue. But, unashamedly it seems; man cannot wait for these natural processes to work in relation to Earth's remarkable systems. Hence, waters that were supplied for steam locomotives were far from pure. Thus, for that reason, curing was the order rather than meaningful preventative measures. At the 'Brick' though, there were water treatment facilities. The plants in operation purposefully softened and purified the water, but their result was purely of a curative nature. Curative treatment is still an increasingly accepted therapy in all spheres of our present system which governmental idealisms are powerless to prevent.

However, to ensure an acceptable measure of steam production, the boiler was subjected to a regular inspection and curative programme. Scale and other organisms, despite the water softening, brazenly invaded the internal super-structure and subsequently formulated brown and orange phenomenons, an occurrence that subjugated heat transmission, and was one definite reason why some engines failed to steam effectively.

Records were chronologically filed and referred to, and this assured an appropriate and proper vigil, resulting in an arranged sequence of boiler washing. In view of this demanding operation, an engine fitter first removes all wash-out plugs and mud-hole doors. Then, donned in his usual battledress of protective oilskins and gauntlet gloves, the militant warmonger, in the shape and form of the Boiler-Washer, is then able to approach his important contest of reprisal. Armed with a high-pressured water hose, the tapered nozzle is fired consecutively inside the plug turrets to counter-attack the metamorphosis. The forced cold water was an effective ammunition entering the confines of the boiler stomach and searching out the ulcerous chemistry. It was surprising how much scale and sediment rapidly surrendered to exit through the mud-hole doors.

It was Leonardo da Vinci who wrote: "Water can be healthgiving, unwholesome, laxative, sulphurous, mournful, angry, red, yellow, green, black, blue, greasy, fat and thin". Although perhaps true, the water supplied at B. Arms did not truly acquire all those written attributes; but many of them were adversely prominent in certain circumstances. For example, a priming engine positively agreed with most of what Leonardo da Vinci was saying!

Priming took place if a boiler was either overfilled, or if it was over-due for washout. Under those somewhat extreme conditions; that is when the regulator valve was consequently opened, a combination of steam and water forcibly entered the steam chest. The result was awe-inspiring as well as frightening, for the engine threw up an impressive thunderstorm of angry spew issuing out of the chimney. The uncountable blobs of hot sulphurous water erupted with a fearful roar that showered the adjacent vicinity, which included the poor engine; or others who might be unfortunate enough to witness at close quarters the microscopic denunciation of "Sodom and Gomorrah". The immediate response, as far as the driver was concerned, apart from ducking inside the engine cab, was to quickly open the cylinder cocks, this action eventually soothing the severe belching inside the cylinder chest; until the fermentation finally stopped. Because water is incompressible, it was known that a complete front end of a cylinder casing could thereby be blown out, and even side motions could forcibly bend under the strain. I never experienced such a case myself, but there were always many episodes circulating among enginemen recalling their own painful accounts.

It was very important however, that all scale and sediment be satisfactorily removed. Subsequently, a physiologist of boiler organisms, or a Boiler Inspector, scrupulously examined the strategic confinements. The regions he would observe carefully were those adjacent to stay and tube joints, for these were the worst offenders. Tests proved that those areas mentioned were major factors for creating water leakage. When subjected to normal working conditions, any scale deposits remaining were highly susceptible to cause an uneven heat exercise through expansion and retraction; hence, possible joint fracture. Furthermore, scale that stubbornly refused to submit was forcibly manhandled by using a long steel lance. If this also failed to dislodge the scale, the Boilersmith had no other alternative but to abduct the intruder at the expense of sacrificing one or more boiler tubes, and therefore replace with new tubes.

After an approval of the completed works, all plugs and mud-hole doors were then replaced and secured. The boiler was then only half-filled with water. The reason being, that when the fire was later lit, the expanding hot water supplemented the remaining space which avoided overfilling.

The black carbonaceous substance, commonly known as *soot*, was yet another evil antagonist that purposefully reduced heat transmission. Therefore, another periodical task was that of external tube blowing. This antiquated practice of cleaning tubes with steel rods and spearhead brushes was still very much preferred in the 1950s, although as I recall, a compressed air-gun was often used in assistance.

Some grades of coal produced carbon and char more than others, but at most, this effect was very much dependent on the fireman's shovel and his approach to controlling an effective, or even, an ineffective fire.

For this reason it would be ideal at this stage to consider the chemical association which takes place between the constituents of fuel and oxygen from whence coal burns. Understanding what these natural compositions are capable of, a fireman was surely to be most fruitful and proficient in maintaining a balanced control over correct combustion for the prime benefit of steam welfare.

Carbon and hydrogen are heat producing components of coal. When these two elements unite with oxygen, heat is subsequently generated. Both these chemical energies require a regulated proportion of oxygen to burn completely so as to acquire the maximum benefits of heat evaluation. Although coal ignites at a temperature just over 800°F, to attain a proper and efficient fire on a steam locomotive, a temperature very much higher must be forthcoming, of which oxygen plays the leading role.

Broadly speaking, there are only two types of coal; hard and soft, but the graded qualities varied considerably, demanding topmost skill and direction from the fireman. The constituents of good firing techniques were primarily based on knowing and understanding the emotions of the burning coals. However, on every steam engine, air is delivered to the firebox in two ways: (1) Primary air, which is the most important, issues from under the fire by way of the dampers. (2)

Secondary, or Top Air as it was commonly known, is admitted through the opened firehole doors and funnelled directly on top of the fire under the baffleplate.

The varied qualities of soft Welsh coal that I personally was brought up on, are substantially made up of fixed carbon and contain a very small percentage of volatile matter. Therefore, such coals require a generous inducement of primary air measured through the dampers and the pull by the steam blower. Whilst burning coal, particularly on the running road, it was good policy to keep the firedoors closed between firing. This method obtained a concentrated influx of primary air, but with hard coal, the opposite was true, which inevitably diminished the amount of black smoke through the exhaust.

Volatile matter consists of numerous gaseous compounds known as hydro-carbons. When these compounds burn, they give off a somewhat congealed display of sulphurous yellow smoke. This awful poisonous output is only evident when a fire has been freshly lit, whereupon combustion is not encouraged until the engine itself makes sufficient steam to operate the forced draught by the blower. However, the so-called fixed carbon content is really the left-overs after the volatile matter has been thoroughly consumed, and the evidence is confirmed in the form of coke. If, for example, the supply of air is cut off, perhaps the ashpan could be full, or the fire is excessively dirty due to clinker blocking the passages through the firegrate, then obviously, combustion cannot be completely satisfied. For this reason another gas, that of carbon monoxide will inevitably formulate. When this occurs, about two thirds of heat production is subsequently lost. Not only that, a build up of carbon solids will in turn congest the inner tube walls creating the aforementioned evil antagonist.

Hard coal is very high on volatile matter, so it ignites very quickly and therefore the condition has to be treated far differently to that of the soft coal. Thus, the different reactions rested in the hands of the fireman to judge the best possible techniques to deploy the maximum benefits under the varied circumstances. For the principal purpose of economics, and regardless of the quality or type of coal, a good fireman will establish a good even fire over the grate. Six to nine inches was considered a practical working depth. If the fire was too thin, the forced draught made holes in the firebed, and partly exposed the firegrate. When this happened, a high velocity quaver tantalised

27

the eardrums with a menacing beat, and only enginemen who have experienced the phenomenon will be able to substantiate the piercing sound. On the other hand, if the fire was too thick, primary air was unable to penetrate quickly, then, an uneven combustion, coupled with a definite heat loss ensued with adverse consequences.

From the foregoing we can understand how important it was to recognise the fundamentals and antics of coal burning, and how vital it was to have a sound and purposeful control of the dampers which, by their regulated use, the right amount of 'primary' air could be measured correctly to support combustion of the carbon and hydrogen, whereupon, the right balance manufactured an outward show of carbon dioxide. Although carbon dioxide is a colourless gas, the evidence was normally observed as a bluish translucent emission from out of the chimney, an indication which tells the fireman that combustion is just about perfect and that the fire temperature is at its maximum peak.

Black smoke out of the chimney, should only be tolerated immediately after fresh coal has been thrown onto a well established fire. Once the volatile gases have been exhausted, then only the hydrogenous and exhaust vapours should rightly prevail. This was often seen as the puffy vaporous white cloud which billowed over the train, the result of both hydrogen and oxygen when correctly combined.

It is worthy of note, that the very position of the brickarch also played a major role in assisting the high temperatures desired. The special fire bricks which made up the brickarch above the fire, absorbed and retained the heat radiating from the fire. The clever idea however was to also increase the length of escape the gases had to make before their final exit through the tubes and out of the chimney. The longer diversion, although fractionally longer, was to permit an extra margin to extract maximum heat value from the passing gases.

It will be appreciated, that to accomplish perfect combustion, control was not as easy as it seemed on paper, for very often crewmen had to work in conjunction with forced or uncontrolled conditions, as will be portrayed in chapter three.

At times though, tubes became seriously congested. So a similar method to that of internal descaling was adopted to dislodge consolidated areas, as well as just general sweeping. If soot was permitted to remain, particularly if the engine was taken out of service for any length of time, soon manifested a yellow non-metallic element occurring free or combined with other elements in sulphide and sulphate; compounds that could at their best, burn tubes and boiler plates with serious developments.

To perform the unpleasant task of tube blowing, a Tube-blower, along with his acquired strength and vigour, was employed and quickly promoted to smokebox level. On opening the smokebox door, a confrontation of large and small tubes were thus exposed. Inside a 'Schools' class for instance, there were as many as 240 tubes to clean and blow through. So, complete with overalls and facial protection, the Tube-blower made sure that the gruelling skirmish did not last too long; for within the hour the black and murky dust withdrew its grip and was henceforth immobilized and speedily subdued in the firebox.

As mentioned in chapter one, when an engine arrived on shed after completing a day's work, the first sequence of replenishment was that of coal and water. In addition to that, I will now put into perspective some of the other daily intricacies which were also very essential in sustaining steam provision. The arrangement was commonly known in abbreviational terms as "Put and Prep" . . . (Put Away and Prepare). The interpretation being that, the fire, smokebox and ashpan were three embodiments that had to be cleaned of all waste products that had accumulated during the course of working. On the other hand, preparation was when the engine was supplied a concord of 'top up' provisions for the next trip, of which lubrication was a profound priority.

Putting away; or 'disposal' as it was more typically known, was executed generally by the fireman. The task was uncomfortable to say the least, and certainly, with all modesty, required first class strength and stamina, especially if it was a hot or windy day. The traditional method of cleaning the fire composed of three so-called fire-irons. These steel tools were customarily kept secured safely on the tender adjacent to the coal and were often buried when taking on fresh coal. A tank engine on the other hand, provided a more convenient space one side, and atop the water tank. Cleaning the fire first required a clinker shovel or scoop, as most preferred to call it. This was a very heavy and cumbersome brute of about nine to ten feet in length, with a shovel-like blade at one end. During the period of cleaning however, the blade particularly became very hot, therefore a cotton wiper, folded in one's hand was an appropriate protection against possible burns. The clinker that had to be removed was really excrescence or slag laver that remained a redundant left-over from burnt coal. This aggressive substance as mentioned, was the guilty agent that mismanaged combustion, and therefore had to be extradited for the continued benefit of steam profit.

However, before the clinker could be removed, especially in tougher cases, the second of the three irons was brought in as a reinforcement. This implement was simply known as the 'dart'. As the name suggests, this long poker-like tool was used for hacking the solid concrete hard clinker into small and convenient pieces for easy access by way of the firehole doors. The third iron was that of the 'rake', or 'pricker'. This very effective instrument adhered a single pronged tooth at a right angle of about nine inches in length. Its function was to lift and drag the broken clinker into position for removal. At times, it was not uncommon to find part of or even whole fire bricks that had inadvertently broken away from the brickarch, then a more detailed inspection of the brickarch was consequently made.

The most congenial method of cleaning the fire was to scoop the good fire over to one side of the firegrate, the exposed clinker was then broken up with the dart and neatly shovelled with the scoop and withdrawn bodily across the footplate, and smartly dropped onto the track side before the fire was again moved over to the clean side for the operation to be repeated. When completed, it was standard practice to introduce a bucketful of stone aggregate to sprinkle at random over the firegrate. This policy allowed the stone to conglomerate the prospective clinker, like currents dotted inside a fruit cake, creating a perforated weakness that made the clinker easy to break when stabbed with the dart. Thereafter, fresh coal was added to supplement the dying embers.

On the more modern locomotives, for example the BR Standards, London Midland types and the rebuilt Bulleid Pacifics, internal drop grates and drop ash hoppers were built-in as a provision for easier cleaning. Although a very good idea in theory, in practical terms the amount of energy deployed left a question mark over the form. In my view, they were not as good as they might have been. More often than not clinker jammed between the bars, and the sweat and toil employed to dislodge the stuff defeated the object, taking as long to clean as the conventional method. On the other hand though, particularly when firing on the main line, the action of disturbing the fire with the rocking apparatus enhanced the attraction of primary air as well as dislocating a clinker build up.

After cleaning the fire, if the same engine was due out within the hour or two, the fireman would then take advantage of banking the fire substantially with large knobs of coal, (each about a foot square). At this early stage, the coal was intricately placed round the back corners and under the fire-doors of hand picked 'cobs'. Sometimes, huge slabs comprised part of the fuel supply, and as was the custom, broken to size. Very often too, large knobs were purposefully placed on the footplate for later use, but the practice was determined according to time, and the nature of the forthcoming trip. The general idea was, not to 'bring her round' too early for fear of blowing off steam which consequently wasted fuel and water.

The firebox of a passenger engine was very capable of scoffing up to a ton and a half of coal, but the fireman had to be very careful not to overload the firebox, more especially underneath the brickarch, for the soft Welsh coal, when well alight of course, had a gruesome habit of swelling considerably, and could thereby disturb, or even worse, 'dislodge' the arch bringing it collectively onto the fire. This was a calamity that would also dislodge words of defilement from the Running Foreman's tongue when he found out! After a satisfying fill of fuel, the baffleplate then commissioned its rightful position comfortably.

Next, the fireman, still streaming with sweat and allsorts, replaced all three fire-irons to their respective place. At the same time he also shovelled a ton or more coal forward from the back of the tender to make up for what was earlier presented to the furnace, and leave a mountain of fist size coal neatly trimmed and readily usable for the next crew. After sweeping and fiercely hosing the footplate with a jet of steam and water, a gentle spray over the coal mountain was highly recommended, especially if travelling tender first out of the depot. Generally though, the footplate was left spick and span.

Our next very important operation demanded both dampers be fully open in order to rake out the ashpan. On each road of 'Old' shed were ashpits. These unmistakable trenches were some three to four feet in depth that were formed between the running rails and provided easy access underneath the engine. Usually the ashpit was ankle deep in water. Because of the many piles of ash and char, it was found necessary to manoeuvre the engine further on or even back to a suitable 'clear' spot before raking out of the ashpan was possible.

Very often there were other locos in front and behind, therefore one had no alternative but to push through the piles of ashes to manipulate a favoured position. However, this unthankful chore required an ashpan rake that was something like the shape of a roulette rake used in the gambling game. After searching for, and finding a suitable rake, the ordeal favoured a crouched stance underneath the engine; with hat pulled down and the collar well up, the hot fine ash was then pushed and pulled out, but not before the swaddling gloom covered one from head to toe with a disagreeable white dust. The taste was equally abhorrent too . . . .

Yet another unthankful chore was that of cleaning out the smokebox. Before opening the smokebox door, a wise fireman closed the firehole doors and gently increased the steam blower sufficiently to pull the hot gases and fumes therein through the chimney. This practice also disallowed cold air from pushing through the tubes as well as avoiding the smoke projecting into one's face when the door was opened. The smokebox interior, depending on the working miles of course, was capable of holding a large amount of char. In fact the fireman had to be very careful when opening the door, as hot char could fall over his feet, and if very windy, the sudden gust prompted the fine granules to lodge painfully inside the eyelids. The firing shovel was used here to throw out the char into the ashpit below. Speaking for myself however, a clean cotton hand wiper was tucked around my neck, and my cycle clips were an effective way to wrap the ankles, but although very helpful, some grit always managed to find its way between clothing and skin. Whilst the smokebox was open, the driver used the opportunity to examine the interior to satisfy himself that all was well. Though rare, 'steam blows' adjacent to the blastpipe and other susceptible parts could well be discovered that could create a mammoth problem when working the engine under stress. If serious, the locomotive was then taken out of commission for repair.

One of the most significant aspects that invited attention at B. Arms was a small mechanical crane that worked slowly, chugging under its own steam astride the running rails. With jib and grab, this interesting machine qualified for the sole purpose of mucking out all ash and clinker that accumulated inside and outside the pits. A truck that was conveniently coupled to the crane was ideal for dropping all waste material into. For obvious reasons the work had to be systematically organized in conjunction with the Running Foreman

Above:
The author at 20 years of age in his mother's garden at Lewisham, in his working clothes and cap.
Above, right:
A typical Bricklayers Arms crew in 1955 with Guard Alf Sandland on the right, on platform 1 at London Bridge. It was Alf who first introduced the author to the railways.

Mercer's Crossing signal box was the first control on the Bricklayers Arms branch from the Motive Power Depot. A signalman always took pride in his box, and all levers and brass fittings were polished as a matter of routine. Even the windows reveal a 'shining' example of cleanliness.
13th November 1954   *R.C. Riley*

An E3 class 0-6-2 'Brighton Tank' No. 32453 waiting at signals at North Kent West signal box at the top end of the Bricklayers Arms branch and waiting to shunt back into adjacent sidings. At this point the road ahead divides; the line to the left goes on past the Rotherhithe Road carriage sidings near Corbetts Lane. The line then ascends steeply to merge into the Greenwich Viaduct and the main Kent coast line (ex-SECR). The line to the right climbs a shallow ascent to meet the main Brighton line (ex-LBSCR) to New Cross Gate. Interestingly the colour light aspect fixed to the signal gantry is the start of the colour light system on the Brighton section. (one yellow or green only).
13th November 1954   *R.C. Riley*

The weeds have taken hold of what is left at North Kent West Junction. The nearest iron bridge carries rail traffic from London Bridge to South Bermondsey station.
10th May 1986   *Author*

The opposite view to the facing page. A powerful three cylinder W class 2-6-4T No. 31919 on full power hauls a goods train against the grade out of 'Sorting Sidings'. The destination headcode is for Norwood Junction. Judging by the shortish train it would appear that a 'banking' engine was not required to assist up the oncoming Forest Hill bank. The class appeared in 1932 as a tank version of Maunsell's N1 class Moguls. Out of the 15 that were built, most allocated to either Hither Green or Norwood depots in the 1950s.

29th March 1958   *R.C. Riley*

A 1986 view of the former North Kent West Junction box, showing clearly that wild growth had now taken over control. No more will the once immaculate signal box control the junction. Both signal box and signal gantry were demolished soon after this photograph was taken.

10th May 1986   *Author*

A Maunsell 'Schools' class, No. 30929 *Malvern* is ready and standing patiently on road 1 of 'Old' shed at Bricklayers Arms depot. These engines were stated to be the most powerful 4-4-0s in the world. Their refined behaviour and exceptional steaming qualities became a firm favourite amongst 73B enginemen. Out of the 40 that were built, 19 of the fleet were at one time allocated to B. Arms. They were principally built for fast running on the impeded Hastings line.
9th November 1954   *Brian Morrison*

Another B. Arms 'Schools' No. 30931 *King's-Wimbledon* taking water on road 5 of 'Old' shed. The crew make sure she is well topped-up before proceeding light to Charing Cross to work a passenger express to Hastings.
2nd April 1955   *Brian Morrison*

A Bulleid 'Battle of Britain' class 4-6-2 No. 34077 *603 Squadron* shows off its full head of steam on road 3 of 'Old' shed. This locomotive was in effect a 'scaled down' version of Bulleid's 'Merchant Navy', and was introduced on the Southern soon after World War II.
11th September 1954   *Brian Morrison*

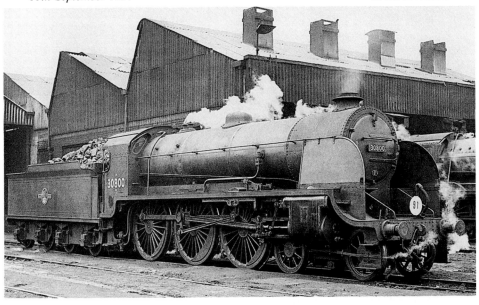

Another Maunsell classic stands formidably on road 4 at Bricklayers Arms. This mighty 'King Arthur', No. 30800 *Sir Meleaus de Lile* was just one of three Bricklayers Arms allocations in the 1950s. The mountain of trimmed coal on the eight-wheeled tender, plus the white plumage of steam suggests it won't be long before it works the Continental ferry vans down to Dover.
14th March 1959   *R.C. Riley*

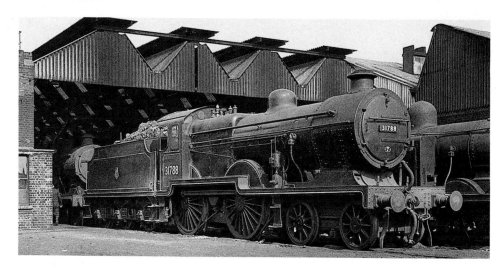

A sturdy looking Maunsell L1 class 4-4-0 No. 31788 stands quietly outside the foreman's office. These engines were a development of Wainwright's L class and were introduced in 1926. Going by the white ash on the tender handrail and steps, it appears that the fireman who cleaned the fire was left handed. The sash window to the foreman's office gave him an excellent view of the coal-stage and the comings and goings of all engines. The shed code at the bottom of the smokebox door (73A) interprets a Stewarts Lane allocation.

2nd April 1955   *Brian Morrison*

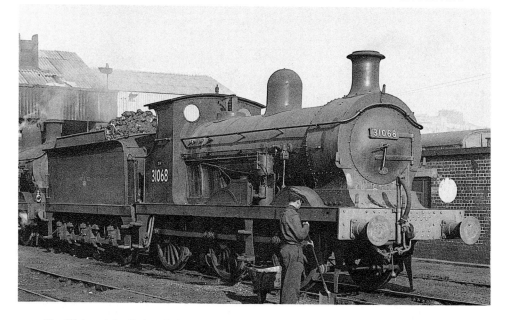

The Wainwright C class 0-6-0 was a powerful and reliable work-horse primarily built for heavy freight traffic. No. 31068 is seen here on road 7 at Bricklayers Arms.

21st February 1960   *Lens of Sutton*

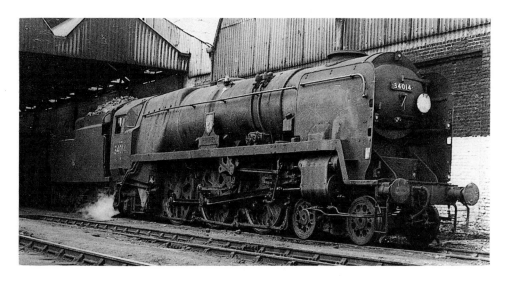

A somewhat dirty looking rebuilt 'West Country' class 4-6-2 – just one of seven assigned to B. Arms in the late 1950s. Although no date is given when the photograph was taken, the white square at the bottom of the smoke deflector warns of electric wires above, therefore, we can conclude it was in the early 1960s, probably just prior to the depot's closure in 1962. That would also explain the filthy appearance.

c1961 *Lens of Sutton*

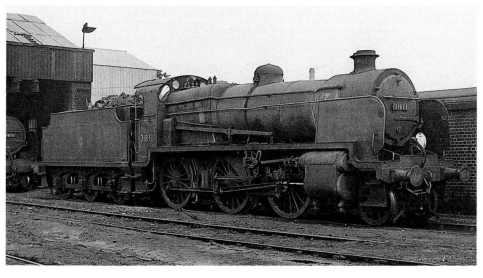

A two cylinder N class Mogul presents itself on road 8 of 'Old' shed. Maunsell introduced the class in 1917. Although ideally suited for freight traffic, they were often commissioned for use on passenger services, particularly on summer specials and excursions. Having only 5ft 6in driving wheels they still produced a tractive effort of 27,000lb, and their bark was as great as their bite!

c1958 *Lens of Sutton*

Here we have a stranger in the camp as far as Bricklayers Arms was concerned, E2 class No. 32107. The Brighton built tank engine is positioned nicely under the coal hoist waiting a refill. The electrically operated lift was capable of hoisting one ton containers which in turn shot the coal at a right angle through the opened hopper, seen above the engine cab. One of the skips can be seen in front of the engine buffers standing on its own narrow gauge track.

Lens of Sutton

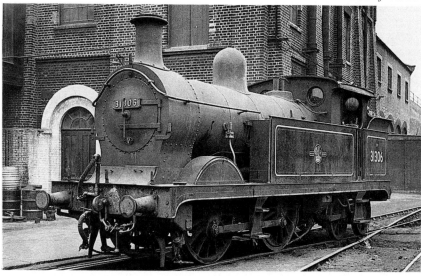

Wainwright H class 0-4-4T No. 31306 is seen outside the oil stores on the approach road to the turntable at Bricklayers Arms. No sign of human habitation – not even a whisper of steam, so perhaps the turntable is in use! These small but powerful locomotives were used successfully on many and varied pull-and-push services throughout Kent as mentioned in chapter seven.

14th March 1959

R.C. Riley

'West Country' class *City of Wells* is receiving attention in Bricklayers Arms repair shop. Increased traffic and a modernisation programme during the early 1930s resulted in a series of new developments including a new repair shop. Incidentally, No. 34092 is now preserved in full steam glory on the Keighley & Worth Valley Railway with numerous outings on the main line.

2nd April 1955   *Brian Morrison*

Disowned and derelict the Bricklayers Arms workshop and turntable as found in May 1986. Interestingly, the floor area inside the workshop is laid over with tar blocks, typical of the 1930s.

19th May 1986   *Author*

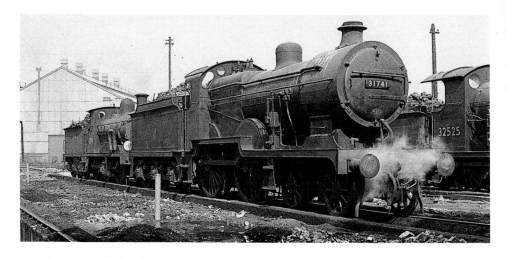

An inside-cylindered D1 class 4-4-0, No. 31741 standing over the pit on road 5 at the back end of 'Old' shed. This area was the main section for disposing of engines. The piles of clinker and ash ascribes that fact convincingly. The repair shop in the background overlooks the scene. C class No. 31294 and C2X No. 32525 accompany this "convert".

2nd February 1955 *Brian Morrison*

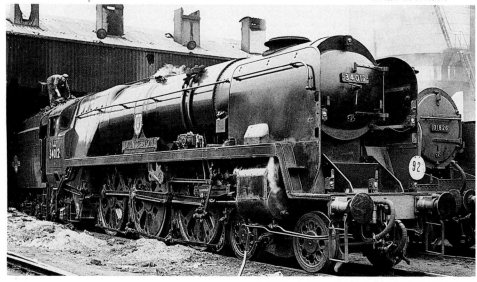

A rebuilt 'West Country' Pacific, No. 34012 *Launceston* stands proudly on road 8 facing the (out of sight) turntable. These engines were installed with built-in drop grates and ashpans. The picture shows clearly the right side ash-hopper, between the rear driving wheel and smaller trailing wheel. When the hopper was full, a steel bar released the contents onto the track side and pit. It appears that the fireman is making safe, larger lumps of coal. Worthy of note is the tall water treatment plant sighted beyond the smokebox of N class No. 31826.

14th March 1959 *R.C. Riley*

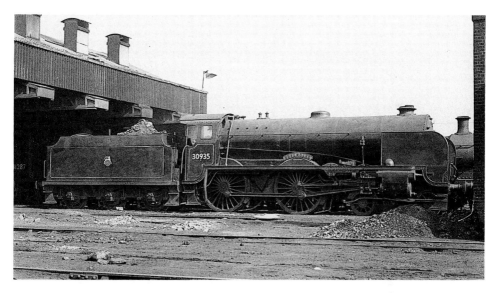

A Bricklayers Arms 'Schools' on road 5 of the 'Old' shed displays a prime example of a 'mountain' of coal prepared for use. Notice too, the fireman's water hose slung over the cab side. No doubt it will be put to good use when No. 30935 *Sevenoaks* travels tender first to either Charing Cross or Cannon Street stations.
2nd April 1955   *Brian Morrison*

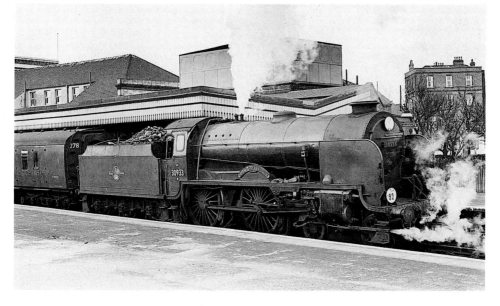

The beautiful sight at Margate station of a 'Schools' announcing it has plenty of steam to spare. Notice the neatly trimmed coal piled high on the tender, a sure give-away that No. 30933 *King's Canterbury* is about to start her journey to Charing Cross via the Dover route. The fire-irons too, are neatly tucked alongside the coal.
28th March 1959   *R.C. Riley*

This picture shows a typical example of a tail lamp that was required by railway policy, to be fixed to the rear of a train to identify its completeness. The same statutory practice went for an engine travelling light too. Of further interest, Sheffield Park Station, Sussex has been preserved as it was in steam days. It provides a beautiful venue for many locomotives in steam, reminiscent of the 1950s and well worth a purposeful visit.

30th April 1955   *R.C. Riley*

The conspicuous headboards seen on the front of 'Schools' class No. 30929 *Malvern*, identifies to all signalmen the train's destination. Here we see *Malvern* in full-cry pounding on the 'down' main line near Chiselhurst. The white discs exhibit the Hasting's route via Tonbridge.

21st April 1951   *Brian Morrison*

Behind the "Man of Kent", seen passing platform 3 at London Bridge station, is the railway medical centre. The sheltered footbridge seen above the train connects directly into the building. Periodically, all enginemen were required to visit the so-called "Harley Street" venue and submit to a rigorous medical examination. The eyes particularly were meticulously tested for signs of colour-blindness. A Bricklayers Arms crew always prepared the "Man of Kent" and was subsequently relieved at Charing Cross station by Dover men who then worked the train back to Dover. Here we find No. 34098 *Templecombe* heading the express.

13th March 1957   *R.C. Riley*

Sharing the scene in this picture of Bricklayers Arms is the cleaners' lobby. This was the place where I spent twelve months as a cleaner boy during 1953. The flat-roofed brick building looks quite respectable from outside, but inside it was not exactly a place of hygiene! The smell of paraffin and stagnant oil, was far from wholesome. The "Vulcan" C2X No. 32551 standing on road 6 was a powerful operator and used quite extensively on the Brighton section. Although, as I recall, the C class was much preferred for comfort and a smoother ride.

2nd April 1955   *Brian Morrison*

The new steel and asbestos roof at Bricklayers Arms is here seen as a much improved structure that spans the complete shed. Even the 'Schools' bathing gloriously in the sunshine shows off its new green livery. Judging by the steel board fixed to the 'Schools' behind N. 30929 *Malvern*, the cleaners are probably busy shining the new livery and polishing the brass name plates with brick dust.
28th February 1957   *R.C. Riley*

Here we have ex-LBSCR E4 class 0-6-2T No. 32471 simmering on road 5 of the 'New' shed. Although capable of hauling light passenger stock, the E4s were more popular on shunting duties. The dented contraption slung to the cab side is the pump that pressurised the air to work the Westinghouse brake system. Often, without warning, the pump decided to stop working, resulting in loss of brake power. With a spanner or the coal-pick the fireman clouted the thing to re-start it. The picture reveals a coal-pick conveniently placed near the engine number.
28th February 1957   *R.C. Riley*

Class E6 Brighton Tank No. 32408 is seen at work shunting one of B. Arms branch sidings, (probably Willow Walk). These later models had so-called 'pop' safety valves fitted with an air-assisted gear lever which spun like a Spitfire propeller! The continuous steam and oil bombardment from below the steam pump has turned the connecting rod a sickly yellow on the rear end.
14th March 1959   *R.C. Riley*

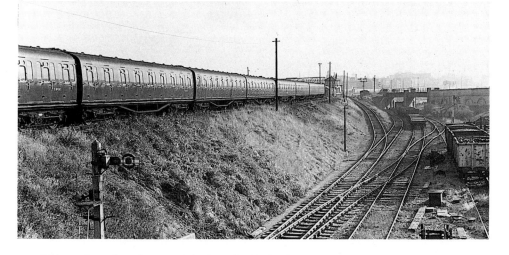

This section of track started the Deptford Wharf trip. In the distance, at the end of the berthed electric train, is the old elevated signal box. To the left of the signal box one can just observe the new footbridge specially built to carry the shunters safely across the permanent way to the 'down' sidings. Just beyond the signal box are the derelict remains of what was the New Cross Gate loco sheds, which had closed in 1951. The steep bank shown here from the signal box descended at 1 in 90 and turned swiftly under the main London to Brighton line (out of picture). It was more like a 'big dipper' than a conventional line.
15th November 1964   *R.C. Riley*

The Deptford Lift Bridge as seen, looking south towards New Cross Gate. It appears that No. 32417, E6 class 0-6-2T is having an easy time doing a spot of light shunting. Immediately to the left of the white fence the Surrey Canal is just visible. The whole bridge was raised by means of a framed construction mounted on four corner posts. The small wooden signal box to the right controlled both rail and canal traffic.
29th March 1958 *R.C. Riley*

A driver's view looking south finds the overhead mechanism of the bridge has been removed. Notice the line ahead splits into three. It was the centre road that rose steeply (1 in 70) to the Gate 'down' sidings. An E6, hauling anything up to 30 laden coal wagons from the wharf, had to plunge over the Lift Bridge at something like 40mph in order to maintain momentum to climb the oncoming bank. On the skyline is the London to Brighton main line.
October 1963 *G.H. Platt*

who permitted a section of road to be clear of engines for the crane driver and labourers to manoeuvre comfortably. Road Nos 4 to 8 of the 'Old' shed were basically the regions primarily used for disposing of engines.

After the laborious work of disposal, the fireman then set about the easier task of preparation. This ensured that all essential equipment necessary for the trip was available and correct. A mandatory list of vital effects are as follows:

Firing shovel, bucket, handbrush, coalpick, small hammer, set of spanners, flarelamp, gauge glass lamp, spare glass tubes/ washers, box of 12 detonators, two red flags, three headlamps and three headboards.

Most of the equipment is of a self explanatory nature, but for the benefit of those who do not readily identify the less obvious items, let me explain their purpose. First the flarelamp. All engines carried at least one flarelamp, but it was very often that two became part of the logistics. The shape was like a small tea-pot, and from the spout protruded a thick stringed wick with its tail curled and soaked in paraffin. Unlike the clean and polished Aladdin's lamp, the black and battered variety provided on a steam locomotive equally proved its worth, particularly at night if the train was stopped at signals for any length of time, the lighted lamp illuminated the way to the signal telephone or signalbox, to contact the signalman for reasons for the delay. Its usage was also very handy when the driver examined or oiled the engine in the dark.

The two gauge glasses positioned on the boiler face, gave a tangible equation to the boiler water level. The glass tubes that were protected behind a toughened glass box were subjected to the full boiler pressure, and although breakage was rare, it was possible for a tube to burst suddenly. If this happened, then live steam and water invaded the complete footplate complex with a resonant uproar. The experience was traumatic to say the least for the brave crewmen, after having been frightened half to death amidst a nil visibility of scolding steam, then had to also struggle to find the stop cocks to arrest the harassment. After isolating the burst, the fireman, with perhaps burnt hands and wet clothing fitted a new glass tube, and the spanners earlier mentioned, provided the means for that operation. Hence the reason why spare tubes and their washers had to be carried.

Another important part of the outfit were the detonators. These were used mainly in connection with emergencies as outlined in the British Railways 1950 edition of the Rule Book. Detonators were approximately two inches in diameter, round shaped and half an inch thick, and adhering to two lead straps for fixing to the running rail. The Rule Book was issued to every engineman. The book showed in specific terms what to do if detained on the permanent way. In fact Rules 55-60 were considered the most important, as far as emergencies were concerned. At the firing school which I had the privilege to attend, George Russell and Fred Brown were both instructors and qualified drivers. During the course of their teaching, one very outstanding method was enforced, that "repetition is truly the mother of retention", for the aforementioned rules, especially Rule 55 were time and again emphasised for our benefit, and I became fully convinced of that.

To explain the purpose of the detonators, nothing could be better than to quote one or two helpful remarks from the pages of the rule book. Rule 57 for example, paragraph (a) has this to say: "Detonators are used for the purpose of attracting attention of the Trainmen. They must be placed as nearly as possible in the centre of the rail, and when fixed by hand they must be securely fastened by bending the clips round the upper flanges of the rail". Rule 59 also explained how a driver was to act on hearing an explosion of detonators at fixed signals or signal boxes, for paragraph (a) says: "When one or more detonators are exploded by a train at stop signals or signal boxes, the Driver must immediately bring his train to a stand".

In the depot however, as far as detonators were concerned, in the preparing of the engine for the next trip, the defined instructions of Rule 58 were thereby conformed to, for it said: "Detonators must be carefully handled as they are liable to explode if roughly treated. They must be kept in dry places and not left in contact with brick walls, damp wood, chloride of lime or other disinfectant, nor exposed to the action of steam or other vapour. The month and year of manufacture is shown on the label outside each packet and is stamped on each detonator. Detonators must be issued in the order of the dates stamped on them; those of the oldest date being always used first". Therefore, ensuring a minimum of twelve detonators, I always made sure they were safely stored in the fixed tool box well away from the damaging effects of those mentioned in Rule 59.

During the course of daylight hours, code destination headboards were dutifully adopted. The white boards, about the size of an above-average dinner plate were positioned on fixed brackets situated each end of the engine, six at the front, and six to the rear. However, before leaving the depot it was necessary that the fireman arranged the destination headboards to the desired positions. The code arrangement on the South Eastern and Brighton sections were of a universal interpretation that specified a deliberate route. For example, if an engine was scheduled to run light engine to Hither Green, two headboards were placed, one top centre, and the other bottom centre, but if running light engine to Grove Park carriage sidings, the top centre and right middle was the fixed positions.

During the hours of darkness, obviously the oil lamps then provided an illuminated destination code. On the other hand though, a very important and yet compulsory rule was that whenever engines ran light they had to carry a rear fixed tail light whether it was day or night. The very presence of a rear lamp indicated to a signalman that the train was complete. If a fireman forgot to position a tail lamp, then the signalman must rightly assume that the train is not complete, then take the required steps to stop the engine and inform the driver accordingly. The guard must also ensure that a red tail lamp is in position to the rear of his train to indicate its completeness, otherwise the same procedure befalls the signalman.

As far as lubrication was concerned, different types of oil was thus required, depending of course on the class of locomotive being oiled. But whether it was superheated or saturated, lubrication was carried out by the driver as part of the preparation service. On the larger passenger engines there could be more than fifty oiling points to attend and top-up. The work occupied the best part of one hour. First and foremost, the driver had to obtain a requisition from the Running Foreman, which was an order to draw a measured supply of oil from the stores. Each engine was equipped with three metal oil bottles of differing sizes for the purpose of immediate identification. The larger always contained the engine oil, the second size for the cylinder oil, and the smallest contained the paraffin for the fireman's use, as I will mention later.

In cold weather it was often a practice of some drivers to place the cylinder oil bottle precariously in the mouth of the firehole. The idea was to allow the heat from the fire to thin the treacle-like oil for easier pouring into the cylinder receptacles and lubricator. On odd occasions however, the bottle and contents did a disappearing trick, but the chimney, on presenting a sudden black cloud, revealed its whereabouts. The real problem now for the driver, was *how* to explain to the foreman a good reason to acquire more oil!

The sight feed lubricator that was subsequently filled, was operated by direct steam from the boiler, the steam displacing oil through several nozzles that were themselves immersed in water. Special observation windows were then able to show how much oil was dispensed to the necessary parts. The steam lubricator could also adjust the oil feed to provide the desired amount, or even shut off the supply according to running conditions.

For the much thinner engine oil, this was used for re-filling the oil reservoirs principally situated on the footplate. Here, the oil was conveniently conveyed by a number of thin copper tubes like long roots pushing out from the reservoirs to gravity feed the bearings by syphon and capillary attraction. Oil reservoirs were also sensibly fashioned and built-in as part of the side connecting rods, where the oiling point was usually corked with a porous cane stopper to permit air to enter to prohibit possible air locking.

Again, for the purpose of preparation, yet another fireman's duty was to clean and top-up the oil lamps with the paraffin, trim the wicks, and indeed light them if required. The same went for the smaller gauge lamp too and after its cleaning and filling, it was then neatly hooked over the water gauge steam cock and rested comfortably one side of the gauge glass to provide the light for sighting the water level in the boiler.

Now sand was another useful commodity that had to be checked during the course of preparation. The steam-operated sanding gear, that was controlled from the footplate, was for the sole purpose of strengthening grip for the driving wheels. Its usage was particularly beneficial when starting away with a heavy load, or with wet and slippery conditions, as it was very likely under those exceptional circumstances, that the driving wheels were subject to slipping. There were four sandboxes on the 'Schools' class, one for each driving wheel. The fireman therefore, after obtaining one of the purpose-made sand buckets filled it with sharp sand. The sand had to be perfectly dry to be effective and for that reason a coal furnace was situated in the building adjacent to the stores and served the purpose well, so there was always a good supply readily available when needed. But no prizes are offered here for the reason why the sand gentleman answered to the name of "Sandy".

From time to time, because of dampness or other defect in their workings, some sandboxes had to be completely emptied. Unfortunately, the fitters did not re-fill them again, not that it was their job to do so, but on these occasions to fill each engine's sandboxes could be a real feat in itself. The sand bucket, when filled, could weigh anything up to fifty pounds or more, and from ground level had to be lifted bodily onto one's shoulder and carried perhaps two hundred yards, if the engine happened to be standing at the top end of roads 5 to 8. On staggering under the weight, the bucket was then heaved above the head onto the engine gangway above the driving wheels. After another awkward scramble to climb the engine, balancing like a tight-rope walker with no pole it was then possible to pour the sometimes burning hot sand into the sandboxes. You may well imagine that if that same procedure was multiplied ten or even more times, one would feel as if Henry Cooper had punched the living daylights out of you in his boxing ring just across the Old Kent Road, but thankfully those occasions were not very often.

This chapter could not be complete unless I mention, with due recognition, the work of the Engine Cleaner and his battle against the forces of dirt and grime. Cleaners were usually boys fresh out of school and cleaning steam engines was really the first step in a humble beginning to that of becoming a true aristocrat of steam, namely the noble Engine Driver. After passing a most rigorous medical examination at the British Railways so-called "Harley Street" venue off number one platform at London Bridge, the somewhat beleaguered young man singularly independent, had to report to the Shed Chargeman. Perhaps it would be appropriate to recall my own brief encounters when I started as a raw cleaner-boy at the 'Brick'.

On my first day at Bricklayers Arms I was introduced, along with two other new lads to Mr (Tommy) Tupper the Shed Chargeman. At first impression he seemed a nice sort of gentleman, but then, the glint in his eye suggested to all newcomers that first impressions may not always be true.

After acquiring our overalls and the black Rule Book from the stores we then followed Mr Tupper to a large notice board displaying all the shed rules. Each of us individually read the rules out loud, a regular formality for all new employees. The need to observe the rules was demonstrated on many occasions, and the notice was a constant reminder of its importance. These written instructions, broadly speaking, encouraged discretion and behaviour in any forseeable circumstance, and to take all work seriously, for the lack of attention, fooling around and the taking of chances ran a risk that could cost lives, not only of oneself, but of others too.

Entering the small brick 'cleaners lobby' that was situated at the top end of road 8, the stagnant smell of oil and paraffin, and the exceptionally dirty seat lockers were far from benign. I quickly realised that I and other new colleagues had to endure these conditions for the ensuing year.

The first important rule that was explained, was that before the cleaning of any engine commenced, the wheels had to be firmly 'scotched', and a red rectangular hand board fixed to the outside lower lamp bracket, with white words which read: "NOT TO BE MOVED". Shortly thereafter, the chargeman produced a white chit for us to obtain paraffin and a bundle of cotton waste from the stores. These were our cleaning materials that helped remove the opaque filth from the 'Iron Monsters'. I well remember my first cleaning job was that of a squalid looking N class that seemingly had not been near a cleaner for many a month. However, whilst we three lads set about cleaning the beast, it was not long before our nice new protective clothing was covered with grime and oil. A stylish comment from a passing driver, recognising the fact that we were babes in the 'Brick', shouted an informal cockney message: "Aye yoo lot, don't forgeta scrub the coal and clean inside the chimney will-ya!".

Over the weeks and months that followed we found "Old Tupper", as he was called unknowingly to himself, a good sort really, as long as the work was done, there were no complaints. Of course, once or twice he had good reason to chase us out of the canteen, or creep up on a group playing cards on the footplate of a dead engine at the bottom end of the carriage shed. But, looking back it was all good fun while it lasted, but most importantly, as far as I was concerned, learning the many functions and features of the engine, as well as the whole ecology of the Bricklayers Arms Motive Power Department, put me in good stead for the future, as well as understanding the struggle every associate had, to keep the 'Iron Maidens' rolling along.

3

Anxious Moments Around the "Arches"

One of the most remarkable projects in British railway history must surely have been the construction of London's first railway, the London to Greenwich line completed in 1836. This outstanding achievement for that era must compare favourably with at least one of the "Seven Wonders of the World". It was George Walter and Colonel George Landmann RE, who were the prime initiators of this mammoth project.

However, before the four miles of double track could be laid, it was planned to erect an elevated plateau of well over 800 brick arches for the purpose of securing a level road with very little variation, for those existing locomotives were not powerful enough to cope with uneven surfaces. Accordingly, the first brick was laid on 4th April 1834, and amazingly, the work took only two years and eight months from start to finish. When the big 'open day' arrived on 14th December 1836, the overwhelming crowds were embraced in a rapturous ceremony of flags and banners while a military band pounded out a well rehearsed flavour of pomp at the London Bridge terminus.

The immense viaduct inflicted a straight scar across that agricultural countryside of Bermondsey and Rotherhithe. Whether one loved it or not, it must have provided a spectacular sight before the Industrial Revolution and human habitation obscured its beauty, the inevitable result of historic development and social change.

One of the ingenious recommendations put forward was to 'let' the hundreds of empty arches for tenements, shops and warehousing facilities. The promising ambition would hope to earn extra revenue to recoup some of the £1,000,000 already spent on the project. Henceforth a few dwellings were incorporated for housing accommodation, but the objective misfired and failed to attract the expected interest. Well, I ask you, "Who wants a train rumbling o'er the roof when you're trying to sleep?".

To accommodate the seemingly impossible operation much land had to be acquired. Protests were many and from far and near. But, in reality, the old squalid and slum dwellings were some of the worst in Europe. Their removal proved to be a blessing, and no doubt the huge numbers of rodents were also glad to move to cleaner and better surroundings – poor things.

The new railway provided a main-spring from the City to within easy reach of South East London, offering a simple journey in minutes, rather than hours by road. This stretch has since become the largest network in the world.

By 1844 a new branch line was merged into the viaduct of Corbetts Lane, Rotherhithe. It was primarily built to serve the new Bricklayers Arms station which opened on 1st May 1844. From the outset the new London terminus failed to attract any real impetus or substantial benefit. The popular London Bridge station nearby verified that convenience was enough reason for most passengers. Nevertheless, with shrewd determination extensive gestures were made by the negotiating machinery; their efforts to reduce train services and reduce fares proved to be disappointing. Thereafter the railway authority accepted defeat and subsequently withdrew all passenger services by 1851. The next time Bricklayers Arms station was used for passenger travel (apart from a few Royal Specials) was to support the war effort of 1914. The all-human stock were contigent male groups attired in military garb, with customary leg-wraps, destined for the front lines in Europe.

The only alternative for the complete Bricklayers Arms complex, without destroying its already dented image, was to enlarge the locomotive depot and branch facilities to provide a consistent and well balanced 'goods' service. History has shown that from the 1850s through to 1930, the extensive freight interactions had affirmed a worthwhile proposition. Also, because of increased traffic and modernisation potential during the 1930s and onward, another series of developments came into effect and was henceforth carried out. For example a new repair and service shop was built which served as a useful vantage point for local repairs. A new 70ft hand-operated turntable was also part of the improvement programme. This table was a must to ably turn the much longer and heavier locomotives. Even the 'Old' shed was provided with a well-deserved facelift and was covered with a complete new steel and asbestos roof. A far cry from the old heavy timbered purlins typical of those earlier years.

After nearly 120 years of rugged yet loyal service, Bricklayers Arms finally closed in 1962, to make way for the tormenting muscle of electrification and dieselisation. Gone too were countless treasures of steam experience, generations of men whose memories remain buried in the archives of time, never to return. But one thing must be certain, all steam crews going back to the 1840s operated over and under the aforesaid 'arches' throwing out their own distinctive smoke and hissing steam. So, on behalf of all bygone enginemen at the 'Brick' or elsewhere, I will now share a few of my own authentic exploits as just one crewman who had the unique privilege to be just a small part of the last generation of enginemen who steamed over and underneath the arches.

Graduating from Cleaner to Passed Cleaner in 1954, it was railway policy to be placed in the "as required" gang. This consisted primarily of shed duties which involved preparing engines for their next duty. When a loco arrived on shed, very often the crew were on overtime and therefore requested immediate relief. Waiting shed crews were then authorised to take charge and perform the necessary chores as explained in Chapter Two.

Over the weeks and months that followed, I gained much valuable experience. Many local and varied shunting 'turns' were locations which afforded instruction for teaching new firemen all aspects of railway procedure. This enforced a close and purposeful co-operation of all personnel, which in turn inculcated a high standard of efficiency which validated railway safety. Shunting signals for both day and night, along with audible signals in fog, were just a few of the formalities learned. The foregoing outlines will explain the shunting 'codes of practice':

Light Signals at Night
1. A white light moving from side to side slowly:
move toward the light
2. A white light swung toward and back from the body:
move away from the light.
3. A green light held quite still was:
slow down, invariably a red light followed to stop.
4. A red light: to stop.

Audible Signals in Fog and Falling Snow
1. One whistle denotes: go forward (toward shunter).
2. Two whistles: to set back (away from shunter).
3. Three whistles: to stop.
4. Four whistles: ease couplings (ease up).

ALL RIGHT

CAUTION OR
SLOW DOWN

DANGER
OR STOP

MOVE AWAY

MOVE
TOWARDS

CREATE A
VACUUM

Hand Signals During Daylight Hours

1. Either arm moved across and towards the body represents:
   move *toward* the shunter
2. Either arm moved in a circular motion away from the body:
   move *away* from the shunter.
3. One or both arms raised outstretched above the head:
   to *stop*.
4. Either arm stretched horizontally with only one hand moving up and down:
   slow down/caution

Qualifying as Fireman in 1955, I was now a classified name in the bottom link to be used hither and thither as a spare man. Of course that was the normal procedure, and really the third stepping stone from that of cleaner, and thereafter promotion to engine driver.

The so-called "as required" duties were by far a long way from routine as far as time and drivers were concerned. For instance, a week's duty might begin at 12.05am, perhaps a local shunting turn; the following day a 3.15am start would not be unusual, maybe to work the 'Tattenham Goods'. A long lie in bed the next morning to commence at 7.00am bound for Deptford Wharf working heavy coal trains to New Cross Gate. A 12.15am start might complete the week in grand style, to remain in the depot as spare fireman with every opportunity of being sent away, perhaps to work the Hastings or Brighton paper train down. It did so happen that on one occasion while I was busy cleaning the fire on a mighty 'King Arthur', the Running Foreman (Jim Foote) came sprinting across the 'Old' shed. Climbing halfway onto the footplate he shouted anxiously above the noise of steam: "Leave that Robert, get yer things and go with Driver Nibbs on the 'Schools' on seven and work the Hastings paper train down will yer? . . . 'cause' is mate 'ain't turned up . . . the idiot's gawn sick . . ." Pouring with sweat I eagerly set off, hoping in all hope that the senior link foreman would remain sick for the next fortnight!

My first rostered driver was Ernie Cole. Ernie was well atuned to railway life, notching at least 40 years service and countless gallons of beer to his credit. While I struggled to drink one pint, Ernie took delight in swallowing three! But then most enginemen enjoyed their pint of 'wallop'.

I was looking forward to the evening shift with Ernie, for he nearly always let me drive. We were assigned to shunt the New Cross Gate sidings, and later bank a coal train up the Forest Hill bank. Banking a train however means assisting the leading locomotive by 'pushing' the complete train from the rear.

Leaving home in good time, I cycled five miles from Blackheath to the depot. The October air was quite cool and the long sponge-like clouds were soaking red from the setting sun, suggesting that darkness was looming quickly. Arriving at Bricklayers Arms, I leant my bike against the messroom wall along with the other bicycles. On entering the long corridor to sign the book, Foreman Fred (SOS) Gregson was prancing down the passageway to stipulate work proposals for the waiting shed crews. Hands tucked firmly inside his overalls he beheld my fast approach. Gripping his pipe between his teeth, creating a screwed up facial deformity, then with much difficulty said: "Yer engine's on one – the Brighton Tank outside the office . . . tell Ernie when 'e gets 'ere she's ready for sailin'". With his eyes to the floor he continued his walk towards the lobby humming and puffing from his smouldering object.

Brighton Tanks (0-6-2T) were powerful work horses and ideally suited for their purpose of shunting, as well as making short hops with either goods or passenger stock. Later models were fitted with an air-assisted gear lever which proved advantageous for speedy shunting, but when one altered the percentage thereon, it was highly recommended to stand well clear, for the heavy steel handle had a natural mannerism of spinning like a top and was capable of breaking a hand if one was foolish enough to leave it in the way. One other problem I found was that they usually jammed at the end of their propelled spin, like a wedge held in a tight grip. The only possible way to free the handle was simply by brute force.

The brakes were operated by a Westinghouse compressed air system, and were very powerfully effective, as they needed to be. The automatic steam pump that pressurised the air was conveniently situated on the fireman's side and fixed to the external framework, easily reached from the cab. The pump was controlled by a governor set on the steam supply pipe. A pressure gauge, which was secured on the boiler face, registered the air pressure. At most though, their temperamental attitude enforced a regular vigilance which was frustrating, to say the least. Periodically, they objected to pumping, resulting in complete loss of brake pressure. When they did stubbornly stop, a clout with a spanner usually got it going again. One reason perhaps why the mule-like 'thingummybob' was traditionally dubbed 'the donkey'.

Leaving the depot with me as driver and Ernie as stoker, we entered the branch line towards the brick viaduct, arriving at New Cross Gate, some three miles on. On this occasion Ernie decided to pop off and whet his appetite at the local pub while I carried on shunting: "Yer know what to do young Bob", was his farewell comment. Most drivers let their fireman 'have a go' as driving was termed; but not many drivers trusted their mates on their own, which was right of course, but Ernie having implicit confidence in my ability knew I would manage okay. After all it was only an hour or so shunting and he would be back – well before the 'banking' job.

Observing the crash of the 'dummy' (ground signal) I reversed the engine from the station platform into the slip road and on towards the 'down' sidings. In the distance I saw a shunter's white light waving me back. High on the darkened skyline, above the shunter's head, I could not help noticing a familiar outline of a 'Schools' class 4-4-0 hauling an 'up' Kent express speeding atop the brick arches heading for London bridge. The distinct orange blaze from its fire gloriously illuminated the night sky, like a shooting star in slow motion. Simultaneously a plain, old London Transport tube train from Whitechapel dashed noisily past me, terminating its journey at the Gate station, its screeching brakes letting everyone know it was coming to an abrupt halt.

The shunter stopped me just clear of the points opposite the water column close to where a Vulcan built C2X (0-6-0) was standing coupled to a complete coal train. I recognised the driver as Wally Court, the Bricklayers Arms branch secretary, who represented all Bricklayers Arms' members of the ASLEF Union. His fireman was busily preparing the Vulcan for the heavy slog up the bank, 'but surely his actions are premature . . .' I thought. Climbing aboard, the shunter announced, for a reason I cannot recall, "There's bin an alteration in the schedule matey . . . yer gonna bank the Waddon Marsh train in fifteen minutes okay? Where's yer mate?" he questioned curiously. Quicker than an instant my brain negotiated my tongue to stammer forth nervously: "Oh, um . . um . . 'es gawn ter make the tea ain't 'e . . . 'e won't be long!". Thankfully he slipped away in the dark, hopefully suspecting nothing. "Cor, luv-a-duck . . . what should I do now?", I said to myself. Ernie would not be back for at least an hour and there was no possible means of contacting him.

Fortunately the darkness was on my side, and no-one I hoped, had any idea that Ernie was in the pub. Anxiously pondering I knew an urgent decision had to made. Should I reveal Ernie's whereabouts or take a chance and bank the train on my own. My imaginary dialogue was by now working overtime, swaying my thinking first one way, then the other. If found out the consequences would indeed be grave, especially for poor Ernie. A reprimand? A suspension? . . . or even worse, the sack! Finally I convinced myself there was very little chance of being discovered; in fact the only person who may unwittingly spoil things was Ernie himself. He could return while I was away. Wrongly perhaps, I chose to bank the train, but my immediate responsibility must be the fire preparation. Understandably the existing fire was rather dismal for we contemplated light shunting for at least two hours, therefore, anything but a large fire was quite sufficient, it was just a matter of enough steam and water to keep the wheels rolling along.

I confidently increased the engine blower and opened the damper wide. Affording a lavish supply of coal, I closed the fire door to get maximum heat. Prudently I hung the storm sheet on the fireman's side to stop the guard peering in, for when the train trundled by it would no doubt obscure his vision, or any other eyes for that matter. Then according to standard practice, I secured two red lamps to the rear lamp brackets positioned over each buffer, and one white light fixed to the front centre bracket. More coal was thrown liberally around the firebox followed again by a quick slam of the door. At that moment, without warning, the guard poked his head over the cab door. My heart leapt a triple somersault and smashed into my rib cage. "Where's the driver cocker? . . . he asked loudly above the roar of the blower. Repeating the same 'tea story', I added convincingly, "What's the load then mate? . . . I'll tell Ernie when 'e gets back . . . 'e shouldn't be long". Satisfied with my presentation, off he went towards his brakevan. I now noted the steam pressure had crept to maximum, 'Lovely' I thought. I opened the fire door and the white glow decorated the enclosed cab. Easing the blower, I decided to add a few more shovelfuls – but only under the door for good measure.

Executing a vengeance against the heat, the safety valves roared; but I dared not put the injector on for fear of priming whilst banking as the boiler content was then nearly full. My eyes once again covetously searched the distant station, hoping in all hope to spot an elusive figure like Ernie, but nothing – only the same noisy tube train I had seen earlier, fast approaching on its return, under the arches and onwards to Surrey Docks and Whitechapel.

A distant whistle from the Vulcan caused the coal trucks to jolt hesitantly forward with every coupling straining the sudden yank. Again my heart pounded, kicking my innermost parts. 'This is it . . .' I thought, swallowing my Adam's apple, fearing that someone might notice the 'one man crew'.

The 'dummy' ahead was off, bidding Driver Court free passage onto the local line. Peering ahead, I noticed the C2X's wheels dramatically slipping and sending up an opaque storm cloud with a smell to match. Skilfully, Wally stopped the wheel dance and enforced a rapid bluster that would conquer the ensuing climb. Just yards beyond the station lay the start of the long upward haul.

I had of course banked many trains before as driver, but never without the second man. Forest Hill bank was no picnic, nearly four miles of a steep 1 : 100 ascent with no let-up, and nothing much more than 20-25 mph could be expected with such a heavy coal train.

The left signal at the platform end was clearly green, beckoning our challenge. 'It's far too late to change my mind . . . I have to go whether I like it or not' I thought. Ensuring the gear lever was in forward motion I released the hand-brake. A little touch on the regulator muted the safety valves as I gently advanced, waiting for the guards van to clear the points. A clear road! I now opened the regulator in an attempt to catch the ongoing train. Edging nearer, the pace suddenly seemed too quick, but I knew I dare not brake. I closed off the regulator to reduce speed, and the safety valves once again blasted a revolt, and the 61 tons of steel and steam smacked unrestrained into the guards van with a "clonk". 'Oh dear, poor old guard, not my best effort' I thought ashamedly. Out of concern, I was oblivious to the guard waving his white light to ease me gently onto the buffers. Thankfully all went reasonably well.

Immediately on connection I 'opened her out' (opened the regulator wide) to sustain the thrust. Once again the safety valves silently took a back seat. Abruptly the exhaust spewed aggressively as the engine took hold of the dead weight. The rapid sequence of buffers clanging along the train told all that we were well and truly pushing. My well-rehearsed whistles, two customary 'cock-a-doodle-doos' conveyed to Driver Court that his rear assistance was now under way. A distant 'cock-a-doodle-doo' acknowledged that Wally received the message loud and clear.

On past the station, the long dark cutting continued, engorging the train from both sides. The Vulcan looked altogether angry, for red hot coals ascended and descended offering a colourful firework display. Because of the precise stress, my own steam pressure fell back to 110lb, 50 below capacity. Gladly the water held its own, bobbing nicely in the top nut, so no immediate worries there I thought.

It was becoming clearly evident that in my concern, the coal I had earlier fed was not sufficiently combusted and was thus provoking the current loss of steam. Taking the rake, I urgently disciplined the raging fire. The black external congealment corroborated my thinking as we pounded onward at 20 mph. Further on, the steam pressure was at last gaining, but the water was by now way down the glass, so I could no longer postpone the water supply. Instinctively I operated both water and steam injector valves. The sweet 'whine' of the opened clack valve turned my anxiety to rejoicing knowing the boiler was now receiving a belated water delivery.

Surveying the whole situation, I checked that the coal trucks were still transfixed by my pushing, but then the thunderous exhaust endorsed my scepticism. No need to worry I thought, and another backward notch on the gear lever could not do any harm, so I held the handle against the spin.

Both green lights at Brockley (local and main line) shone piercingly through the smoke and sparks of the Vulcan exacting a green apparition. A disguised but reputed green feather also declared that Wally's stoker was having a good trip, but then, to be fair, he did have a superfine start, knowing the immediate demand.

I peered through the fire door tilt flap. The white hot inferno was satisfactorily combusted and requested more. I obliged, spreading at least six shovels-ful over the box. Black clouds once again shot out, but pouring with sweat, I could not tell whether it was fear from my dilemma or purely physical exertion, maybe both. Producing the rake again, another feel through the fire showed that more coal was necessary, I obliged accordingly.

Having now passed Honor Oak Park, and despite the arduous toil, the steam pressure endured a healthy sign above 150, 'old clever clogs' I thought, smiling to myself. The water too was at a satisfactory level, halfway up the glass. What could be better I thought, except perhaps for Ernie to be by my side!

I could now well afford to relax the injector, but only for a short while though. A couple of more spoons of coal and she was steaming

A somewhat rare sight for the population of Eltham Well Hall. No. 30800 *Sir Meleaus de Lile* is diverted via Eltham and Dartford to pick-up the Chatham line at Rochester, probably with a day excursion. The oldish, eight carriage stock being hauled is an easy load for the might of the 'King Arthur'.
30th May 1959   *Lens of Sutton*

A wonderful view of Borough Market Junction signal box situated between London Bridge and Cannon Street stations. No doubt the signalman was kept busy, particularly during rush hour periods. The straight line to the left carries on to Charing Cross while the right hand curved section passes a brewery before entering Cannon Street. Notice too, a small portion of the lower roof to Southwark Cathedral on the far right.
20th March 1955   *R.C. Riley*

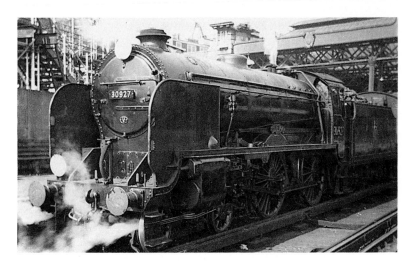

Platform 5 at Charing Cross station sees 'Schools' class No. 30927 *Clifton* at the head of a Folkestone 'flyer'. *Clifton* was the very first 'Schools' I fired on the main line. The steam plumage from the safety valves explains noisily that there is 220psi on the steam gauge. Although no date is given as to when the photograph was taken the larger cabside numerals indicate, the early 1950s. From 1956 most 'Schools' were re-painted in green livery and smaller numerals were adopted.
c1955   *Lens of Sutton*

Festival of Britain year finds No. 30903 *Charterhouse* ready for the 'off' to the Kent coast. From platform 5 the photographer has taken an interesting shot of Hungerford Bridge with its steel latticed side elevation. The elevated signal box is of particular note and which gave signalmen a picturesque view of the 'Dome of Discovery' and other amenities featured on the South Bank. Often a fireman made the tea in the signal box before the trip.
24th March 1951   *Brian Morrison*

Rebuilt 'West Country' class No. 34021 *Dartmoor* sets off in earnest down the slight grade on platform 3 of London Bridge station, and the start of the Greenwich Viaduct. The dome of St Paul's is unmistakably visible on the top left.
14th May 1959   *R.C. Riley*

This was the place of the Lewisham train disaster on a foggy night in December 1957. This so-called 'temporary' structure replaced most of the original flyover. Not exactly a pretty sight, but a stark reminder of those who perished on that tragic night.
May 1986   *Author*

Here we have rebuilt 'West Country' No. 34027 *Taw Valley* pounding against the grade on the 'down' local line at Hither Green. Hither Green loco sheds are situated behind the tail-end of the immaculate looking green Bulleid carriages.
2nd May 1959 *R.C. Riley*

Again on the 'down' local 'West Country' Pacific No. 34097 *Holsworthy* is just about to haul the red and cream Bulleid stock into the darkness of Elmstead Woods Tunnel. Noteworthy, are the destination name boards on the roof of each carriage. On this occasion it would appear that Margate, Broadstairs and Ramsgate could be the appropriate display, for one mile beyond the tunnel the train will diverge left to St Mary Cray and onward to Chatham and the seaside resorts. The rich looking trees are the first definite signs of Kent's green and fertile land since leaving the London suburbs.
11th May 1954 *R.C. Riley*

No definite sign of a white feather but plenty of black smoke; perhaps the fireman is experiencing a rough trip. Having just passed Grove Park, 'Schools' class No. 30908 *Westminster* is seen on the 'down' main line approaching Elmstead Woods Tunnel. The square looking custom built stock suggests the train to be Hastings bound. The reason for the purpose-made carriages is explained in chapter six. For the record, the electric train emerging from the tunnel is a Sevenoaks to Charing Cross commuter.
11th May 1954   *R.C. Riley*

'Schools' class No. 30933 *King's-Canterbury* ascends the 1 in 100 Sole Street Bank on the 'up' line to London. In the distance the delightful Med Valley stretches across Strood and Rochester at the foot of the bank.
11th July 1953   *Lens of Sutton*

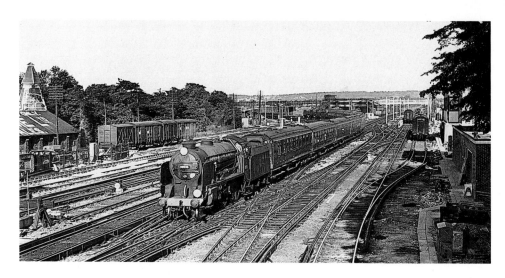

The splendid sight of a 'Schools' hauling a train round the bend at Faversham. The locomotive is No. 30938 *St Olave's* on the 'up' main line. Notice the driver leaning out of the cab preparing to stop the train at the station (out of picture) At Faversham, as the picture clearly shows, the road divides; the left line from whence No. 30938 has come, takes a north east route hugging the sea to Margate. The right route takes a more direct line to Canterbury and Dover. Certain trains from London were separated at Faversham, whereby the front half went on to Dover. An engine from the nearby loco depot was waiting to couple-up to take the rear portion to Ramsgate. A few engines are just visible by the shed, situated at the extreme rear of the train.

13th June 1959   *R.C. Riley*

A few yards east of Whitstable station remain this side elevation of what was once an over-line bridge for the line from Whitstable to Canterbury. The six mile long, single track line was built as early as 1830 and was one of the world's first railway projects. A steam locomotive was bought from Robert Stephenson, but the new engine, *Invicta* could not get through Tyler's Hill Tunnel because its chimney was too tall.

14th September 1986   *Author*

Projecting 1920's design is Hastings station although actually built in 1931.
14th September 1986   *Author*

Waiting at Ramsgate depot is 'Schools' class No. 30910 *Merchant Taylors*. Sadly, the depot closed in late 1960, but here No. 30910 (Ramsgate-based 74B) appears to be ready to work a train to London via the Dover route. With electrification pushing for complete supremacy, *Merchant Taylors* was probably one of the last 'Schools' to work in Kent.
March 1959   *Real Photographs*

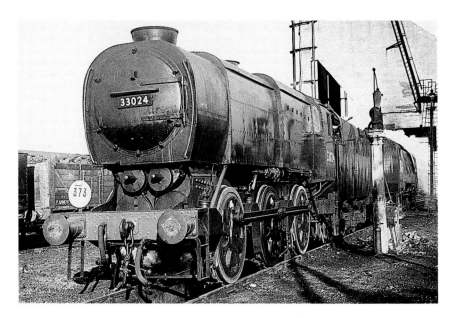

A Bulleid Q1 class 0-6-0 No. 33024 on Ramsgate shed. Forty of these 'out of the ordinary' engines were built during the Second World War. Due to the war effort, national economics were of paramount importance, and therefore, Bulleid had also to tighten his belt. The so-called 'austerity Charlies', although looking externally bare, did not lack power, producing a 30,000lb tractive effort.
2nd February 1952   *R.C. Riley*

An impressive sight as a Bulleid 'Merchant Navy' Pacific hauls the famous all Pullman "Golden Arrow" to Dover. She is seen here pumping out a beautiful stench at Sydenham Hill before plunging down hill through Penge East Tunnel.
26th May 1951   *Lens of Sutton*

A Bulleid 'West Country' class pounds under the main Chatham line near Bickley.
The awe-inspiring exhaust trail impiously saturates the over-line bridge. No. 34104
Bere Alston, was a 'scaled down' version of the nine ton heavier 'Merchant Navy'.
20th February 1953   *Brian Morrison*

Bromley South station is the venue for 'Battle of Britain' No. 34089 *602 Squadron*
seen here climbing the bank to Bickley Junction. This class was identical to the 'West
Country', only the subject matter of the names being different. Both the 'West
Country' and 'Battle of Britain' locomotives contended the Southern scene soon
after the Second World War.
25th May 1958   *R.C. Riley*

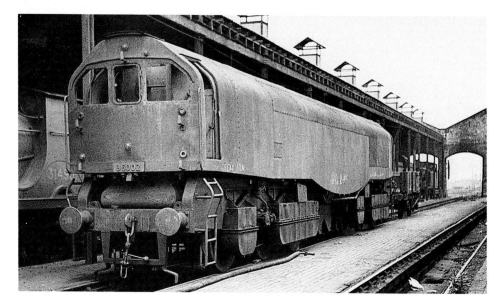

An unimpressive sight of the ambiguous 'Leader' class, the last of Bulleid's productions, with No. 36002 seen here at New Cross Gate waiting to be scrapped. Only five were produced, and because of their failing endeavour, all were scrapped in late 1951.
23rd June 1951   *Brian Morrison*

A Gresley A4 class Pacific sweeps smoothly near Finsbury Park near journey's end from Glasgow to King's Cross. The Pacific is non other than No. 60022 *Mallard* which holds the world speed record for steam traction. The streamlining refinements of Gresley's engine seemingly rubbed off on Bulleid, for before coming over to the Southern as Chief Mechanical Engineer, Bulleid worked with Sir Nigel on the LNER. Comparing Bulleid's Pacifics to that of Gresley's, one can see just a hint of the latter's personality.
11th May 1954   *Brian Morrison*

Heading a Folkestone "flyer" is 'Battle of Britain' class No. 34079 *141 Squadron* on the 'down' main line at Chislehurst.
22nd September 1956   *R.C. Riley*

Driver Bill Marsh is leaning against the side motion of rebuilt 'West Country' class No. 34012 *Launceston* at Ewer Street Continental depot. He was an enthusiastic driver and certainly knew how to handle a C class with a loose coupled train.
June 1958   *Author*

A close-up view of the butterfly fire-hole doors on a Bulleid Pacific. Easily noticeable but not easily manageable above the fire doors, is the steam-operated device which was worked by a foot-pedal on the floor (just below the fireman's arm in the picture). It was far simpler to use the hand-operated handle as shown.
(This photograph was taken on the preserved 'West Country' No. 34092 *City of Wells* at Haworth loco shed in Yorkshire.)
16th May 1987   *Author*

Approaching Petts Wood 'Battle of Britain' No. 34080 *74 Squadron* dominates the scene. Against the sultry sky a tall cavalier feather endorses a maximum spirit. The black smoke explains that the fireman is feeding the ravenous beast to maintain the pressure whilst on the climb to Knockholt.
13th February 1954   *Brian Morrison*

Expressing its wrath against the grade, 'BoB' No. 34066 *Spitfire* hauls a Victoria to Ramsgate express between Bickley and Chislehurst. Five and a half years later the same engine was the major recipient in the Lewisham rail disaster.
17th May 1952   *Brian Morrison*

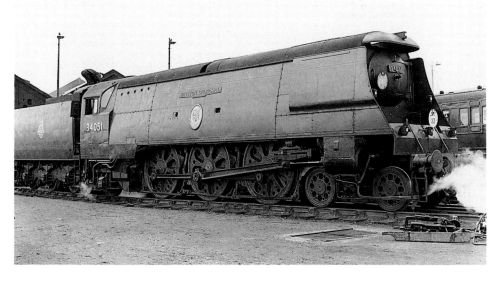

All 'Battle of Britain' class locomotives were named after Royal Air Force squadrons, or names applicable thereto for their efforts in defeating the German "Luftwaffe". For example our picture shows No. 34051 *Winston Churchill* at Salisbury, named after the wartime premier for his prodigious performance during World War II.
May 1953   *Real Photographs*

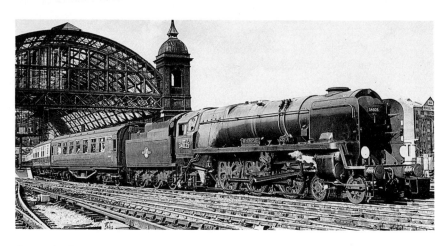

A new-look 'West Country' class pulls out of Cannon Street station, Ramsgate bound. From early 1958 60 of Bulleid's twelve year old light Pacifics were rebuilt. Gone were the old sealed oil bath that the internal chain driven motions splashed about in, their impracticality exposed malfunctory symptoms. Even the steam gear lever was replaced in favour of the screw and drum type. Three sets of Walschaerts valve gear were also installed. Our picture shows a fine looking specimen in the shape of No. 34025 *Whimple*. Of added interest, high up inside the crescent steel roof, scaffolding has already been erected to remove the bomb damaged canopy.

30th May 1958   *R.C. Riley*

Rebuilt 'West Country' class No. 34012 *Launceston* at Cannon Street station, about to haul empty Bulleid stock to Rotherhithe Road carriage sidings. In the centre of the platform a steel gantry is very evident. This was part of the apparatus that eventually removed the complete roof. The youthful fireman looking at the photographer is the author.

June 1958   *Author's collection*

Looking well-groomed and sophisticated, rebuilt 'Battle of Britain' class No. 34088 *213 Squadron* stands coupled to an equally *en grande tenue* train waiting at Tattenham Corner station for the 'royals' to return from the Epsom races.

Lens of Sutton

Rebuilt 'Merchant Navy' class No. 35009 *Shaw Savill* in mint condition hauling at least 13 'bogies'. The summertime express is seen here at Andover Junction on its way to Waterloo from Exeter on the South Western section.

July 1957   *Real Photographs*

Pulling heartily away from Ramsgate station is 'Schools' class No. 30915 *Brighton*. The old black livery, and the absence of the third conductor rail suggests the early 1950s period. The station reception building is prominently visible in the right background with its tall arched windows. Noteworthy too, is the tall gas light beside the first carriage. The engine head-code interprets a Victoria destination via the white cliffs of Dover.

6th April 1953   *R.C. Riley*

Looking black and uninviting is Shakespeare Tunnel. The twin bore tunnel was cut through and the work initiated by Sir William Cubitt in about 1840. The portals of Normandy architecture begin a straight stretch of 1,387 yards under the chalk cliffs.
18th June 1987   *Author*

Standing formidably above Folkestone is Foord Viaduct. There are 19 arches shaped from 100 feet high brick piers, yet another colossal accomplishment by Mr Cubitt. The view from the train atop of the viaduct looks over the harbour and town centre before sweeping into Folkestone Central station.
18th June 1987   *Author*

like a good 'un. Here and there the left embankment was burning profusely, and light smoke ascended over Beadnell Road (where I used to live eight years prior, with still no signs of the 'Bogie-man'). The hot cinders and rocket bombardment inevitably burnt the wild growth; it was a common occurrence and could not be avoided. No doubt the local fire fighters from Perry Vale would soon be busy attempting to rescue the burning weed.

Putting the injector back on, I also wound the gear lever forward to enchance the grand finale. Numerous rockets flew high to match the Vulcan, two firework displays now freely available for the residents of Stanstead Road, for at this point the railway presented an elevated view.

Reaching Waldram Crescent bridge indicated the hard slog was now over, so I eased back the regulator to permit the couplings to stretch little by little with the pull of the leading engine. Once through Forest Hill, the fireworks display had now ceased, and the level track accelerated our speed above thirty. Up front, Wally knew only too well that momentum had to be maintained to avoid a breakaway, so I could not afford anything to go wrong now, and a divided train would surely put the sparks amidst the dynamite. All I had to do was gently hang on to the buffers, no pushing to the other side of the station; stop, wait for clearance and return to the Gate.

The guard by now had already hung his three red lamps to the rear of his brakevan, and the platform lights watched him screw his handbrake a firm touch in order to grab the coal wagons and so preserve the couplings' tension to thus avoid a snatch.

My eyes met the water level as I closed off the regulator. Instantly the water disappeared from sight but exposed itself again, finding its own level one inch above the danger mark, thank goodness! A double pip on the whistle told the signal man of my lone presence. The coal train had by now absconded under the footbridge towards Sydenham. Strictly in conformity with the 'code of practice' the guard and fireman exchanged a waving white light to say that all was well. In the distance the yellow glare of the Vulcan lit up the puffy exhaust trail which violated the chestnut trees off Dacres Road before disappearing from view.

Coasting past the dummy signal I lifted the brake handle. 'Oh bother . . . goodness me', and all that – nothing happened! In my plight I had not noticed the steam pump had stopped, thereby losing complete brake pressure. My response automatically wound the gear lever full back, bruising my hand in the bargain. I then opened the regulator a firm touch; the unpredicted turmoil caused the engine to knock and wrestle, defying the reverse motion. But joyfully the gear confined a momentary restraint but only to self-propel from whence it came. I screwed the handbrake down as fast as my left arm would turn. Finding mid-gear, I then promptly opened the cylinder cocks to release the steam build-up in the cylinder chest. The engine at last groaned to a halt. 'What a palaver!' I thought, bashing the 'donkey' with the coal-pick, whereupon the piston came to life, hammering up and down for all its worth, pushing the much needed air into the empty cylinder, but slowing to a gentle rhythm as pressure was restored.

The storm sheet was still intact, screening the red brick signal box and others walking along the parallel alleyway. "That's the worst bit over with", I said silently, and wondered if Ernie had returned, hoping for his own good that he had not. Except for the steam pump and the 'sing' of the injector all was peacefully still as I waited for an 'up' "juice train" (electric) to pass before being cleared to return.

Safely back at New Cross Gate, Ernie was nowhere to be seen. Had he had an accident? Was he in the shunters' lobby spilling the beans? I wondered if I had done the right thing.

Halting at the water column I re-filled the water tanks (normal policy) and discreetly removed the storm sheet. Two shunters carrying their poles and lamps came striding over the wooden walkway which was planted across the four-tracked permanent way. They had to cross swiftly before the approaching 'down' express hurtled by.

Ten minutes later, with still no sign of Ernie, the shunting was in full swing. Whilst pulling a raft of wagons towards the Gate station, my eyes discerned the "elusive pimpernel" in the shape and form of Ernie Cole. I breathed a sigh of relief. "Everything alright Bob?" he whispered as he heaved his weight on board. "Yep" I said', keeping one eye on the shunter who then held a red light aloft. The brake application made Ernie grab the hand-brake and the loose wagons ran into each other, provoking a plangent repetition.

However, my later explanation to Ernie transposed his face to the white of the hair underneath his shiny cap. Needless to say, our secret was kept (until publication of this book).

Another somewhat milder episode was when I was fireman to

driver Wally Court. Wally was an 'old Brighton' man with a pleasing sense of humour. Wally possessed a coarse, but melodic chuckle, especially if the fireman was struggling to maintain steam.

For good reasons, I always enjoyed the short but fiery tones at Deptford Wharf as well as a good wholesome breakfast cooked on the footplate. Deptford Wharf was yet another early conquest of railway endeavour and was opened for traffic in 1849. The pleasing location was neatly tucked away alongside the River Thames, very near to where Sir Francis Drake was knighted by Elizabeth I, akin the Royal Dockyard for his activism in playing a game of bowls.

Many coal barges were towed up river and docked at Deptford; in their turn they were unloaded and weighed off into waiting coal trucks. Because of their weight, steam engines were not permitted access to the dockside. Therefore the coal wagons were positioned to and from the river by means of power-operated capstans. Long ropes were thus hooked and looped to haul the heavy trucks against the grade, a distance of about 50 to 100 yards. When adequate wagons were loaded and subsequently weighed, the pilot engine was then commissioned to assist and thereby formulate a train. Then the same engine transported the complete train to New Cross Gate 'down' sidings.

The duty began early, at about 7am. Running light engine to New Cross Gate 'up' sidings, our first undertaking was to haul a train of anything up to 100 empty trucks and take them to the wharf for coal re-fill. The short, sharp trip started from where the derelict remains of the old loco sheds were from their closure in 1951. In preparation, all the fireman needed to do was to ensure a full head of steam and perhaps enough fire to stabilise the steam pressure throughout the mad dash. But, as always, the last 100 yards would provide the crucial test.

Setting off, bunker first from behind the elevated signal box, the single line 'peak and valley' track, just under two miles in length, was more like a 'big dipper' than a conventional railway line.

Slowly approaching the first descent of 1:90, the signalman knew that it was vital we had a clear passage through to Deptford. Establishing full stretch and a wave from the guard, we pursued the zig-zagging course, hanging on and full steam ahead.

Once the link of communication is realised throughout the couplings on full stretch, the driver can only then enforce full throttle. However, that was also determined according to weight and length of the train and, of course, the section ahead. Things became difficult with an extra long train, especially on the Deptford route, as the first half of the train would be on the ascent, while the rear half could still be riding the descent. So whenever there was an up and down gradient with a loose coupled train, the skill of the driver could only be complemented with full co-operation from the guard, and how effectively he was able to manage his brake. It was therefore imperative that the guard, like the driver, had an intimate knowledge of the road and used his brake accordingly. On these occasions the engine and the guards brake were the only means of controlling and stopping the train. Such was the case at Deptford.

Despite the down gradient, Wally now opened the regulator almost full with little cut-off on the gear lever. It was a fearful experience to hurtle downhill on full steam and it was more like a ski-race down a slalom course, because the train was so long, speed was of the essence, not only to sustain tight couplings, but also to use the momentum to wrench the train up the forthcoming 1:70 climb.

Charging past the Millwall football stadium, a right hand curvature took us under the London to Brighton main line. Now at ground level, Wally gave her full throttle with little if any cut-off. The supreme surge would inevitably maintain the coupling stretch and so stop the train running into us. A left hand jolt swept us further on and over an antiquated lift bridge which spanned the Surrey Canal. How that bridge stood up to those daily beatings was beyond a miracle! A hesitant rock over the canal and a long hard look at the steam pressure told me I must throw a few shovelfuls of coal around the fire. With parted legs and curled toes, I managed a comfortable grip to feed the violent creature. I was certain the volcanic blast whipped the fuel straight out of the chimney, like a hungry dragon with no teeth. Wally grinned feebly, holding a dog-end between his lips, smouldering his white moustache.

In full view of Greenwich Viaduct, a slight snatch caused the engine to strain the full weight, a tug-o-war in its true sense. As far as I could see, the rear of the train appeared intact, as the guards van materialised, chasing the last truck under the Brighton Line. The guard was doing an excellent job in holding the brake against our pull, but now he would need to release his brake to strengthen our battle to Deptford.

A right hand bend and the engine lurched and shuddered under the viaduct. The frantic blast from the exhaust inside the long arch not only kept our heads in, but cursed every truck wheel that recorded the intermittent rail joints with a coordinated regularity, a malediction beyond compare. The smoke lingered silently over the viaduct and jostled with a passing "juice " train before disappearing from sight.

Gladly our steam preserved a maximum spirit, and there was no immediate need to operate the injector, not until we had reached the summit, for we required plenty of room in the boiler to enable the engine to remain quiet (not blowing off steam) at Deptford.

Suddenly, and without warning, the locomotive showed to be struggling with every jaded bark. Wally stared at me and then turned his eyes to the steam pressure: 'Nothing wrong there' I thought assuredly. "I bet some stupid clown has left a handbrake down on a truck" Wally uttered with disgust and no longer smiling. His choice grammar was not exactly seasoned with salt, more like black pepper! The bank took its toll, and slowly but surely the engine retired and stopped just yards from the summit, just before Evelyn Street Road bridge. I therefore put the injector on and opened the fire-hole door to stop the safety valves pouring forth their fury. I was far too late, their sudden extravagance brought an old woman darting out of her terraced house below a steep embankment. Her threatening fist and moving mouth was not as clean as the washing on her line. We could not hear her comments above the noise of steam, but perhaps that was just as well.

Promptly, she gathered in her washing, but her white mongrel dog continued his bark, no doubt wishing he could sink his fangs into our lower anatomy. Fortunately, the fence restrained his wild attempt.

Wally then told me to contact the guard and explain the problem, and at the same time check that all the handbrakes were individually off. Low and behold, Wally was right, for I discovered no less than four brakes well and truly pinned down. It was a wonder we had got so far I thought. Releasing the brakes with the guard, I hastily returned to the engine. By this time, Wally turned off the injector, and the safety valves were nicely stilled, though I could not say the same for the white mongrel.

Before requesting assistance, Wally decided to have another bash. Three pips on the whistle told the guard to release his brake. A couple of chuffs and we held our breath, but as expected, the wheels slipped and danced against the drag. The impulsive exertion however, sent rockets and all sorts over the adjacent gardens. I was sure glad Mrs had taken in her washing. The dog retreated, in the hope of not changing into a black spotted Dalmatian.

With the regulator half open, Wally spun the lever in forward motion to ease the couplings. Another swift spin in reverse and the engine gathered enough speed to snatch the train over the brow. This was a formality all drivers used on those occasions.

Barking solidly over Evelyn Street, above the rush hour traffic, we finally descended the 1:130 gradient into the wharf, and the shunter stopped our slow approach opposite the lobby. Wally insisted he make the tea, a rare privilege, while I steam-cleaned the firing shovel to cook a well-deserved breakfast of eggs, bacon and a fried slice. A celebration worth much more than a knighthood from the new Queen Elizabeth!

After breakfast and shunting as required, we headed a train of some 30 wagons laden with coal, an overall weight of perhaps 650 gross tons to be taken to New Cross Gate. Obtaining the right of way, we tackled the impending climb. A chuff every two seconds, with an odd wheel slip reminded us of the extreme weight against the pull of gravity. Reaching the summit, both starter and distant semaphore signals were 'on', forcing us to halt opposite the old woman's house again. No doubt the lift bridge was in use offering canal traffic priority. Our hard slog and glowing fire accelerated the steam pressure and needless to say, the safety valves once again let go an agonistic storm, inviting the same woman and her dog, to again, deliver an equally contentious black melody. Removing her washing for the second time, she stormed inside her quieter abode. Staring at the signal, Wally pretended not to notice, but instead, burst forth in song: "My love's like a red, red rose, that's newly spring in June" . . . Not really appropriate for the occasion.

Ten 'long' minutes later, the crash of the top signal invited us away. Wally opened her out, and at last the safety valves dropped. I splashed the fire generously with coal, sending black clouds over the houses. Glancing back, we noticed the distant signal had by now raised its own arm, inviting a clear run to the Gate 'down' sidings. It was always slow-going for the first 30 yards, because two thirds of our train was pulling back on the wharf bank, but once the guards brake topped the summit, it was full power with gravity to assist. Down and under Greenwich Viaduct, we crashed noisily over the rocking canal bridge at about 40-50 mph. Hopefully our momentum would carry the train up the next bank.

Of interest, the lift bridge was designed so that the whole structure was raised by means of a framed construction mounted on four corner posts. The winching was launched by steel chains, and when raised, provided comfortable headroom for canal traffic.

Immediately over the bridge, the line divided into three roads. The left junction went down to terminate at the fabrication works very near the tall Maziwattee Chimney, a profound landmark for miles around. The right juncture turned under the Brighton line from whence we plunged earlier. Now we were invited to take the centre road that ascended very steeply at 1:70 to finally level out parallel with the wide permanent way. Quite often a Brighton Tank, despite the momentum, just about struggled over the top to reach the siding at about 10 mph. Putting the injector back on we slowly rolled to a stop at the water column for a re-fill.

A few days later, Wally was called into the office to explain the aforementioned event. Apparently, the old woman had, quite rightly, reported her encounter. The conclusion of the matter was that no train from that time on, was permitted to stop on the signal outside the woman's house. All trains had to remain in the wharf and await road clearance before proceeding to the Gate. A satisfactory result for one woman and her dog.

My next account is a series of events which occurred in a space of about one hour.

One afternoon I was booked a local turn with driver Tom Hicks. Tommy was a witty and down-to-earth character who took his job too seriously which, from my point of view, seemed more outstanding than most.

However, Tom spent most of his duties as a motorman (electric train driver) working the mid and East Kent passenger services. In fact, a minority of motormen, in the 1950s, were re-called for steam duties, especially for weekends and extra Sundays. On this occasion Tom and I found ourselves walking speedily from Bricklayers Arms to London Bridge to relieve a Dover crew working an 'up' express from Folkestone. "What yer wearing yer jacket for in this 'ot weather?" I asked Tom with a smile, "We'll be back in the 'Brick' in an hour!" "Well yer never know" Tom exclaimed in reply, "Yer might let the fire go out for me to catch cold". He then pinched my face between finger and thumb, a painful habit I never relished. His tall youngish stance strode quickly onward, as if his life depended upon our getting there. He must have felt uncomfortably hot inside his thick outer garment. "Silly old fool" I muttered with muted breath.

Our short cut brought us near Guys Hospital at the base of several brick arches which began the London to Greenwich Viaduct. The warm sun prefixed a psychological boost to our rhythm, one good reason why I thought it was not necessary to wear my own serge jacket. A few trees appeared radiant pervading the hospital complex. A few leaves fell unhurriedly to earth suggesting that autumn was around the corner. Afar off, over the City, a few clouds darkened the distant sky, an ominous telltale of what was in store.

As I expected, we arrived well ahead of schedule, but then that was typical of Driver Hicks. Whilst waiting on platform 6, an amplified voice disturbed our thinking. The dissonant outcry proclaimed: "The 3.40 from Folkestone is running 30 minutes late" but added a pleasing apology for the inconvenience. "Marvellous 'ain't it" said Tom. "If I wanted to commit suicide – I'd chain me'self to the line and probably starve to death".

Sure enough, and exactly half an hour down, a 'King Arthur' (No. 30799 *Sir Ironside*) clanked pompously at the head of a ten car train labouring to a halt opposite the sloped exit. Doors were flung open, and passengers swelled the platform forcing me and Tom to rush the footplate ahead of the human deluge.

The crew were more than pleased to see us, and briefly related their 'rough trip'. Looking utterly peeved and exhausted, the driver retorted in his Kentish twang: "We had to stop at Sevenoaks for a 'blow-up' yer know (restore steam). How we got through Sevenoaks Tunnel, I'll never know". Amongst other unrepeatables, both enginemen stepped onto the platform. "Don't worry we'll sort her out" I said competently. With that, both men disappeared down the long ramp pursuing a solitary passenger.

The steam pressure gauge was just 10lb below the maximised 200lbs. Even the water level was riding high in the glass! "What was all the fuss about?" I questioned curiously, but then, as I suddenly realised, the last 15 miles into London, which included four miles over the arches, were relatively easy going, by which time the fireman had opportunity to recover his sad state of affairs.

We now had only two miles to Charing Cross, and were then scheduled to transport empty coaches to Rotherhithe Road carriage sidings before running light engine to B. Arms, so no 'real' worries as far as I was concerned. As was normally expected, the existing fire content should suffice until we entered the 'Brick'. For as policy had it, a diminished fire was a good bet for cleaning purposes.

One yellow aspect, the driver's side, invited us up the slight short gradient. By now the porters had emptied the mail van, and all other doors were noisily slammed. The green flag and whistle from the guard enforced the right of way. With his right hand, Driver Hicks pushed the regulator handle from left to right at a downward thrust, across, and just above the fire-hole door knocking the sanding gear 'on' at the same time with his left, but nothing happened. Unlike Tom, he had forgotten to wind the gear lever forward from its existing 'notched up' percentage. Realising his oversight, he wound the lever forward. The engine suddenly 'coughed' and missed a beat before gaining its stride. Eventually, the exhaust exploded and increased its anger over the steel bridge.

High above the Borough High Street, *Sir Ironside* mushroomed billows of white clouds that lingered against a sultry sky. The wheels, for their part, wanted to dance, but the sand refused permission.

It was now raining gently and more storm clouds gathered above the spires of Southwark Cathedral forestalling an air of damnation over the railway. The sun, now ambushed behind a cloud, failed miserably in its attempt to break free the gloom.

The signal, the other side of the bridge, displayed a red light. Immediately on stopping, the same signal flashed to one yellow: "Typical" stormed Tom, blowing the vacuum brake off at the same time. Once again he pushed open the regulator, opposite the Borough Market Junction signal box.

On an 'Arthur', unlike the 'Schools' class, the regulator handle was short and stubby and so, had to be opened at least halfway before movement could be promised.

The rain now bounced heavily on the boiler, and my thoughts bounced to our return journey, and travelling tender first, exposed fully to the rather unpleasant elements. Hopefully, the storm sheet would provide adequate protection I thought. A hard slog round the bend, and Tom thankfully eased off power. It was just as well, for steam pressure had dropped like a stone in a pool of water to below 140lb. Not wanting to feed more coal, I swung the long rake into action hoping to dislodge some clinker to permit air through the stifled fire-bars, but the 'concrete' mass was solidly adhered and the dart was not much use either. My vain struggle convinced me that, for reasons only known at Dover, the fire and ashpan could not have been cleaned prior to leaving Dover shed. The amount of ash and clinker was beyond a joke and could not have been created on that journey of less than two hours. Although there was ample fire, it subsequently lost heat production by being starved of vital oxygen.

A quarter of a mile on, a green light helped us into Waterloo station with only 130lb on the clock. Few passengers got off amidst a lightening flash although for obvious reasons, the distant thunder was not heard. For other good reasons, my stomach made a rumble of satisfaction from the meal I enjoyed earlier; fish and chips bought from the Old Kent Road. Tom's voice echoed across the footplate: "Don't worry Bob, we'll sort her out" he said jokingly, repeating my own earlier comment. "Only over the water (River Thames) and we're home and dry" he added, opening the regulator at the same time. Staring at the downpour, I was not too sure what he meant by the 'dry' bit I thought with a wry smile, but then, glancing at the water level, perhaps he meant the boiler.

Passing the green signal, the platform end saw us off under the station footbridge. Slowly past the Festival Hall, the pressure sank to 110lb, and the water level expressed cause for concern. Although I wanted to, I dare not operate the water injector until we reached the station. We both stared at the two brake needles supporting only 15 inches of brake, six inches below normal. "It's a wonder the brakes 'aven't cum on yet" I said politely, while Tom kept seriously quiet. I wished then, that I had not spoken, for at that precise moment, the brakes began to bite. Unfortunately for vacuum brakes, when steam pressure dropped substantially, the brakes involuntarily leaked on. In a somewhat desperate attempt, Driver Hicks gave it all he could possibly muster, hoping to beat the brake pressure. Under normal conditions, steam would have been shut off at the entrance to Charing Cross Bridge, permitting the train to coast across the Thames to enter the confines of Charing Cross station, but the present affair was far from normal.

Despite Tom's efforts, all was lost. The brake shoes finally and aggressively strangled the pull, halting the green giant underneath the elevated signal box, a few feet from platform 6. So near, yet so far. The passengers now savoured a·wet and soggy view of the Houses of Parliament, providing of course, they could sight the building through the rain and steel girders. From our point of view, it would have been a kindness if the bridge had collapsed for us to enjoy an honourable defeat, swallowed in the depths of 'Father Thames'.

Driver Hicks at once went off to inform the wondering signalmen, to explain why we had run out of puff. From a favourable advantage though, Tom did not have far to go. I continued every possible means to 'bring her round' an expression often used to increase steam, or a 'blow up', as some preferred to call it.

What had made matters worse however, was that the heavy rain filled the firing tray to over-flowing, carrying coal dust onto the footplate. Plus no decent coal within easy reach. Without delay I struggled over the tender to shovel a large amount of coal forward, and was awarded a soaking for my enthusiasm! Desperately I threw fresh coal into the long (9ft) firebox. All we could do now was *wait*.

Thereafter, the minutes went by painfully slowly, wearing our patience. Positively, but lazily, the pressure gained strength and increased to 120lb, but that was still 80lb below maximum. Tom decided to hit the brake handle in order to create a vacuum. Our eyes fixed to the brake-gauge, we saw both needles creep to 19 inches. Well satisfied with that, Tom took a chance and opened her out. Sounding the whistle *Sir Ironside* answered the call and dragged the train forcibly to a stop inches from the station buffers.

Henceforth, we restored an admirable revival of both steam and water. We were now 50 minutes behind schedule, and the empties we were booked had by that time been transported to Rotherhithe Road carriage sidings. By and large, we were now required to remain coupled to our train, whilst another locomotive headed the rear end, which inevitably, became the 'front' end. That arrangement suited us fine under the present circumstances as we could now rely heavily on the fore engine to do the brunt of the work.

I removed the destination code boards and positioned a tail lamp in accordance with statutory practice. Tom suggested I hang the storm sheet before moving off. I agreed wholeheartedly without question for I had no jacket to wear. Opening the tool box I discovered with horror that there was no sheet to hang! "We'll sprout gills before we reach R. Road" said Tom. His brown eyes glanced despairingly at the station roof being bombarded with rain water.

Opposite, on platform 5 stood a 'West Country' class engine waiting permission to go up and reverse onto our train. At length, we departed from the station on a green light. Driver Hicks gently assisted the leading locomotive over the Thames and promptly shut off steam the south side of the bridge, but the rain continued with full power. The cascading 'buckets' forced us both to huddle close to the boiler face to escape the monsoon, but there was no escape.

Two yellow aspects the other side of, the appropriately named, Waterloo, certified our stopping opposite the office block near Ewer Street depot. Creeping casually to a halt, granted us a momentary reprieve from the streaming liquid. Seconds later, a whistle from the leading 'West Country', told us our exemption was now over, and we were thus sentenced to further drowning.

Observing the green light Tommy obliged and strengthened the pull by pushing the empties over the curve, but relaxed the power at London Bridge. The steam and water remained surprisingly healthy as we clanged noisily through the station. On we went over the viaduct and gathering speed and needless to say, generous rains from above. Suddenly, contrary to expectations, a loud bang rocked our soaked clothing. A deafening roar of hot steam and boiling water instantly enveloped the footplate like that of a hot Turkish bath. Visibility nil, we knew what had happened. Although very rare, a gauge glass had burst, ejaculating full boiler pressure. At once, Tom removed his jacket in a vain effort to smother the force, and to protect us both from the scalding barrage. Amidst the blind confusion of burnt arms and jacket sleeves, we finally managed to isolate the two stop valves that were able to stem the screaming crescendo. It seemed likely that rain had penetrated the gauge glass protective box, thereby, the contrasting temperatures had blown out the glass tube, hence our dilemma. Further on, we agreed to replace a new glass in the comfort of the depot.

Moments later and thrice as wet, Tom now took over control and stopped the train behind a signal gantry just north of the North Kent East signal box. Obtaining a clear road and a blast on the whistle, we pulled the empty carriages, together with the 'West Country' from whence we came, but only to pick up the points which directed the train left to enter the Bricklayers Arms branch. Slowly descending, Tom dropped the handle (full brake application) at the foot of the steep bank, approximately two hundred yards in length. I immediately climbed off the footplate and ducked between engine and train to uncouple the 'Arthur'. Soaked right through I climbed back onto the footplate. "Wana borr'er me jacket?" Tom asked. His strained laugh was as deafening as the whistle from the engine, and I threatened to hit him with the shovel.

Thereafter, the adjacent left semaphore signal raised its arm to allow us onward to the depot. Meanwhile, as far as the empty stock was concerned, it was now the responsibility of the other engine driver to propel the train into the ongoing sidings, by which the guard and local shunter directed the blind manoeuvre. When the shunt was complete, the 'West Country' itself would then travel light engine to Bricklayers Arms shed.

Arriving on the coal-stage, Driver Hicks went off to report our dripping predicament while I supervised coal replenishment. Minutes later and with considerable surprise, two men climbed aboard the footplate. It appeared that Tom had successfully persuaded Percy Molyneux (Running Foreman) to relieve us. It was a relief too, from my point of view, for I did not now have to clean that extremely dirty fire and ashpan. No doubt the smokebox was chock-a-block too. I eagerly set off to change into my spare overalls which I kept conveniently safe in my locker.

Dry and comfortable, Tom and I sat in the enginemen's lobby reading the daily papers with "Garth" and "Jane" over a well deserved cup of tea to await further instructions. Sure enough, Percy Molyneux, who always displayed a special appeal and personal magnitude, overshadowed the lobby door. He smilingly said: "When yerv'e drunk that Tom . . . you and yer mate nip up-t' London Bridge again and relieve the Ramsgate men on the 6.10 will yer . . . and take the empties to Blackheath and come back light". I looked at Tom, and we both gazed at "Niagara Falls" washing the outside windows. "I've gotta *'dry'* jacket Tom! . . . yer can borr'er mine if yer like", I said tormentingly. But Tom had the last laugh and produced his heavy railway mac, and joyfully he pinched my face.

4
A 'Schools' Safari in the 'Garden of England'

Nowhere will my theme be more clearly presented than by having the pleasure of your company to ride with me on a live trip and taste first-hand the excitement and tremors of footplate experience. At the same time we will enjoy Kent's broad and spacious acres of lush green meadows of fruit and vegetation, completing the journey at the small but busy seaside town of Ramsgate. Our safari will also include incidental anecdotes that will impart a breath of life to substantiate the text.

We will therefore assume it is a pleasant and warm sunny day, perhaps a Saturday in the early summer of 1959. Our duty is to work the 9.05am 'special' from London's Charing Cross station, and probably one of the last steam trains to operate to Ramsgate, because electrification of the Kent coast was now nearing its completion.

Appropriately, our engine is a 'Schools' class locomotive, No. 30927 *Clifton*. I choose *Clifton* for sentimental reasons, for it was the first ever 'Schools' that I had the privilege of firing. The driver for the trip is my old mate Fred McIntyre with many years experience and certainly well versed with the 'Schools' prolific functions.

We now join our gallant steed, rapturously rich in steam, awaiting our company on platform 5. The eleven carriage train is equally resplendent in its usual Bulleid green livery. The present crew have no doubt spent a lot of painstaking time preparing the engine for the outward trip. An adequate supply of fuel and water, a fine head of steam, and most complementary, a well lit and invigorating fire banked neatly under the firehole doors with plenty around the back corners of selected and hand picked lumps of the soft Welsh grade. A thinnish fire over the front of the sloping grate was quite normal, for the 'Schools' preferred it that way.

Relieving the previous crew at 8.45am allows good time to make the tea in the signal box located above the immediate platforms, some steep steps will carry us to the wooden structure conveniently positioned on and over the entrance of Charing Cross Bridge. Providing we wiped our feet before traversing the clean floor, the signalmen did not mind us filling the teacan with their boiling water. The tea however, was adjudged quite positively a life sustaining liquid on any trip, and one could be absolutely sure of noticing the undisguised manifestation on every locomotive in steam. In fact it was part of the furniture, and was, (jokingly) more of a priority than the water inside the engine boiler!

There was never room for any doubt, that steam engines did, and still do, exhibit a sort of breathtaking wonderment for many people. Such was the case at Charing Cross station, particularly on platforms 5 and 6 that were primarily reserved for steam trains. The fascination of an engine in steam motivated admirers of all ages. Enthusiasts and spotters armed with camera and pad were ever present, like a magnet attracting metal objects. For these reasons, although it was not officially permitted, we found it very discouraging to refuse an excited youngster with his dad glued tightly behind, permission to board the footplate and peer into the red hot inferno and to scrutinize the array of handles, wheels and gauges that controlled its invisible might.

The station shunter, after coupling the engine to the train, requests that Fred 'make a brake' (create a vacuum.) This was performed by opening the brake ejector valve and lifting the master handle vertically to the 'off' position. Simultaneously, two fingers on the brake gauge automatically responded the action. Using a clock face as an example, the two metal fingers, correspondingly equal, one each side, rose from the six o'clock position and resigned at ten o'clock and two o'clock respectively. When the two fingers registered 21 inches, this identified that the braking system was working harmoniously throughout the train.

By now our eleven corridor carriages, securely fastened to *Clifton*, slowly consume a mixed bag of human specimens who hastily examine their own place of refuge and happily look forward to their day out by the sea.

Whilst awaiting the right of way, the guard dutifully acquires the driver's name and home depot. Writing the same in his little black book he readily relates the total number of carriages and their tare weight. Having this informal knowledge is fundamental in knowing just how much power is required for hauling over transversal sections of tight bends and up gradients, as well as braking distance and for stopping the train in the correct place on any platform.

Furthermore, for the benefit of a good trip, I personally made it a regular practice, that before any journey I would inspect the smokebox lugs to ensure their tightness, and at the same time, examine the destination code boards to ensure that they were holding their rightful positions. Of course this routine was no slur on the previous crew, but it was customary to double check.

In addition, lubrication is another vital personality that demanded first class attention. The many oil reservoirs accommodated oil-soaked 'trimmings', made up of Worsted thread that reconciled a metal pin, and together, both thread and pin were simply inoculated in a hole provided to supply oil at an appropriate rate by capillary attraction. On the other hand, to permit a controlled flow of cylinder oil to other major parts, the steam and hand-operated lubricator served the purpose well. This solid brass contraption situated on the fireman's side was generally controlled by him, and once set, it did not normally require any purposeful attention until journey's end.

Charing Cross station and its six only platforms were constructed for the South Eastern Railway in 1864. Sir John Hawkshaw, who was also responsible for the nearby Cannon Street station was the original engineer who fostered control in organising the monumental task. An unfortunate occurrence took place in 1905 when a roof tye snapped, large metal segments of the crescent trussed structure collapsed, pushing part of the western elevation onto the Avenue Theatre, and sadly, six men lost their lives in the fall. The then 3.50pm Hastings train awaiting its departure was also partly covered in the cascading debris, and, for obvious reasons, the train remained a non-starter.

Interestingly however, the station was erected on the site of the old Hungerford Market, and the iron lattice and girder structure that spanned the River Thames was also masterminded by Sir John for the South Eastern Railway in 1866. In view of the foregoing, it was found necessary to dismantle the Hungerford footbridge. Moreover, the two wide brick piers that supported the footbridge were left in position and can still be seen among the round iron pillars that support the now existing Charing Cross railway bridge, which is often referred to as the Hungerford Bridge to this day.

The present transverse ridge and furrow roof that now umbrellas Charing Cross station is not outstandingly conspicuous, the somewhat simple and straighforward construction leaving a lot to be desired, but for those reasons the methodical composition restores the purpose well, and it is surprisingly in keeping with other contemporary and more modern counterparts.

Just about half a mile away in a westerly direction is an

BR Standard 4-6-2 'Britannia' class No. 70004 *William Shakespeare* taking the renowned "Golden Arrow" south to Dover. But alas! the first three coaches are not the customary chocolate and cream Pullman stock. No doubt at this point the train is gathering speed after coming off the sharp bend before Tonbridge, for the next 30 miles is as straight and level as an 'arrow' to Ashford, where speed records have come and gone.
19th April 1958   *R.C. Riley*

The Bulleid Pacific sweeping down the bank towards Bickley station is No. 34083 *605 Squadron* on its last fling to London Victoria. An observant eye will notice the leading coach to be a Pullman.
6th April 1955
                                                                                                    R.C. Riley

Shortlands Junction sees 'Schools' class No. 30917 *Ardingly* hauling an 'up' train which, in a few minutes will be entering the south eastern London suburbs.
27th July 1957   *R.C. Riley*

The fireman appears to be taking things easy as 'Schools' class No. 30916 *Whitgift* glides through Sydenham Hill.
16th May 1959   *R.C. Riley*

Projecting like an upside down oil rig, Battersea Power Station commands a defiant mood, but No. 34099 *Lynmouth*, is in no mood to hang about. The 'West Country' is seen here measuring its speed over the arches at Factory Junction. To the left, under the tall wooden tower, the hazy smog is not a sand storm brewing, but is a continuous cloudbank of fumes from the dozens of locomotives at Stewarts Lane depot.

19th September 1954   *R.C. Riley*

Here we see an ex-Bricklayers Arms 'Schools' class polished and shining in the afternoon sun. The profile clearly shows how Maunsell designed the tender and cab to bend inwards to facilitate the smaller tunnels on the Hasting's route. The scene is on the Bluebell Railway at Sheffield Park where No. 928 *Stowe* is lovingly preserved in her original livery. As soon as the signal comes off, the 'Schools' will haul a train of restored SR stock to Horsted Keynes, just five miles through a culture of green trees and meadows.

14th June 1987   *Author*

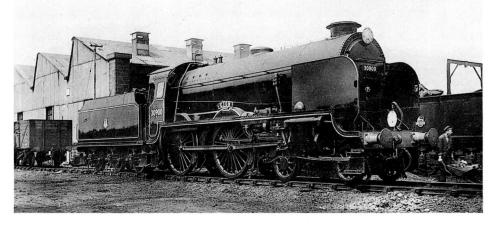

Like a 'black knight' in shining armour, 'Schools' class No. 30900 *Eton* stands proudly at Hither Green depot. *Eton* was the first of 40 'Schools' built at Eastleigh. Although purpose-built for the impeded Hastings line, this locomotive made its debut in 1930 working an express from Charing Cross to Folkestone, while engineers were still carrying out vital track alterations between Tunbridge Wells and Hastings.

24th May 1952   *Lens of Sutton*

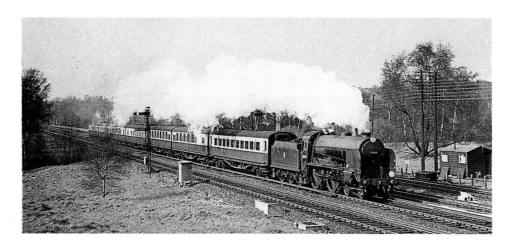

Only seven carriages for 'Schools' class No. 30904 *Lancing* which is seen here striding on its way to Hastings, between Petts Wood and Orpington. Notice the purpose-built stock is slightly narrower than the conventional gauge, the reason being to engage the confinements of the tunnels on this line.
7th April 1954   *Brian Morrison*

The unmistakable baroque towers of Cannon Street station see 'Schools' class No. 30920 *Rugby* setting off at the head of its 'purpose-built' train and one of its last trips to Hastings. Standing in the wings on platform 8 (extreme left) is one of the new demus (diesel electric multiple units). The writing on the wall was fully interpreted for the prestigious 'Schools' empire. In late 1958, the diesel units took over as the new ruler on the notorious Hastings line. Unperturbed by it all, rebuilt 'West Country' No. 34021 *Dartmoor* shoots out a glorious white feather before hitting the trail to Ramsgate.
5th June 1958   *R.C. Riley*

Up from Hastings finds 'Schools' 4-4-0 No. 30924 *Haileybury* vigorously climbing the bank at Hildenborough before entering the dank depths of Sevenoaks Tunnel. Detect if you can, the purpose-made stock chasing through the smokecloud.
23rd May 1953   *Brian Morrison*

Another fine Bricklayers Arms allocation was 'Schools' class No. 30923 *Bradfield* seen coming off the 'down' main Dover line at Tonbridge. Providing the signals were favourable, *Bradfield* would be pounding aggressively up the bank towards the first of the impeded tunnels (Somerhill) on the Hastings line. Worthy of note is the 'scaled' down Pullman carriage, positioned sixth in the train.
19th April 1958   *R.C. Riley*

A splendid confrontation up the bank at Chislehurst. Despite the rapid acceleration, it appears as if the safety valves are going to let-go an almighty roar; such were the incredible faculties of the 'Schools'. Notice too, the Hastings gauge stock in red and cream livery. This 'Schools' is one of three preserved, being No. 30926 *Repton*, recently repatriated following a sojourn in the USA.
26th December 1951   *Brian Morrison*

A celebrated 'Schools' as far as I was concerned was No. 30927 *Clifton*, for she was the first 'Schools' I fired on the main line. *Clifton* is seen here on full regulator against the grade at Chislehurst. The specially made stock suggests a Hastings destination, and the head-code confirms that fact more convincingly.
22nd September 1956   *R.C. Riley*

Like a fish out of water, 'Schools' class No. 30920 *Rugby* is preparing to climb the grade through Tonbridge with a goods train from Ashford to Bricklayers Arms.
26th March 1953   *Brian Morrison*

Making her presence felt, and looking ready for a good clean, is Class V No. 30929 *Malvern*. Pulling away from the slip road at Ashford station it makes its way onto the main line to Folkestone and Dover. The heavy train is of conventional Bulleid stock too wide for the Hastings route.
24th September 1955   *Brian Morrison*

The driver shuts off steam as No. 30928 *Stowe* emerges from the short Somerhill Tunnel on the descent to Tonbridge. In a few months, from when this picture was taken, the sharpened axe of railway technology shut off steam completely on the Hastings line. But the 'Schools' class seen here was exempt from the execution and is now preserved on the Bluebell Railway.
19th April 1958   *R.C. Riley*

In belligerent mood, No. 30928 *Stowe* again, strews out a pugnacious volcano widely over the Kent countryside. Approaching Petts Wood, the headcode reveals a Folkestone destination.
5th May 1951   *Brian Morrison*

Sweeping down Hildenborough Bank like a supersonic peacock, No. 30932 *Blundell's* shows off a flamboyant plumage. Interestingly, you will note the unique high-sided tender. This was for the purpose of holding at least nine tons of coal for special 'rounders', being that *Blundell's* was capable of working from Charing Cross to Charing Cross via Ramsgate and Dover without having to waste time re-fuelling. Here though the 'Schools' is off to Hastings.

23rd May 1953   *Brian Morrison*

'Schools' class No. 30936 *Cranleigh* is seen here hauling a Margate special, passing Denmark Hill. It has yet to encounter the many more London suburbs, such as Peckham, Crofton Park and over the Catford Loop to finally pick-up the main line at Shortlands Junction.

16th May 1959   *R.C. Riley*

Bricklayers Arms-based 'Schools' No. 30938 *St Olave's* emerges from Priory Tunnel and prepares to stop at Dover Priory station, on its first leg to London with an 'up' special relief.
24th September 1955   *Brian Morrison*

One of the offending tunnels that has had both double lines ripped out and centralised by a new single track, to enable a comfortable passage for the '4-CEP' emu seen here emerging from the tunnel, on its way to Tunbridge Wells.
24th May 1987   *Author*

From Tonbridge it would appear that the five mile stretch to **Tunbridge Wells** was a difficult place to reach by rail, and those early railway engineers had their work cut-out in more ways than one. Here is just one example of bridging a large gap near Southborough, this being Southborough Viaduct.
23rd May 1987 *Author*

Tunbridge Wells station is seen here receiving a refurbished "1066" Class 411 '4-CEP' emu, No. 1600 emerging from Wells Tunnel. Although the tunnel remains double-tracked, all drivers have to observe a speed restriction.
September 1986 *Author*

A shining example of a Hastings line train in the so-called "Jaffa cake" livery is seen here stopping at Battle station. The prominent "1066 Electrics" logo sounds-out another electrifying period when William defeated Harold.
September 1986 *Author*

Grove Hill Tunnel is shown here at the opposite end of the station at Tunbridge Wells to the previous illustration. The Hastings to Charing Cross emu is '4-CEP' No. 1525 approaching the platform slowly, for this tunnel imposes a 10mph speed restriction to repel any sway that might contact the tunnel sides.
September 1986 *Author*

An inside-cylindered L class 4-4-0 No. 31781 is shunting back into Faversham station to pick up passengers for Dover.
30th September 1958 *R.C. Riley*

A Maunsell L1 class 4-4-0 No. 31783 is seen picking up the slip road at Crowhurst Junction. The L1s were introduced on the Southern in 1926 to keep abreast with the new generation of railway rejuvenation and came out on top as far as increased power was concerned. This example is seen here hauling nine bogie carriages with a weight of nearly 400 tons.

25th July 1953   *R.C. Riley*

D class No. 1732 looks rather forlorn at Stewarts Lane mpd. Their characteristic 'hump-bridge' wheel splashers reveal the engineering of Wainwright and Surtees just before the turn of this century. Like the L class, many were subjected to rebuilding due to a higher degree of a proposed railway development.

10th June 1950   *Lens of Sutton*

Accelerating magnificently under stress is D1 class rebuild No. 31743 approaching St Mary Cray on a Margate excursion. These so-called 'converts' came on the scene in 1921 and most remained in active service until almost the end of steam traction on the Southern.
14th July 1951   *Brian Morrison*

Pulling vans away from London Bridge (low level) station is a D1 class No. 31735 on its way to Dover via Chislehurst Loop. The dome of St Paul's is again prominent in the background.
14th May 1959   *R.C. Riley*

At Bricklayers Arms shed E class No. 1547 stands opposite the coaling stage. This was just one of the older 'breed' that remained in operational service despite the rebuilding programme in the 1920s.
10th June 1950   *Lens of Sutton*

A weight restriction at Holborn Viaduct meant nothing heavier than a "convert" was allowed. The picture shows E1 class No. 31507 coupled to vans for Chatham and beyond. Judging by the headcode, the train will take the Catford Loop.
1st May 1954   *R.C. Riley*

ostentatious building projecting a flamboyant clock that rings a famous bell above the "corridors of power". Understandably, the familiar drawn-out chimes of "Big-Ben" are not heard on platform 5, for the engine noise drowns out all external sounds.

A few fat pigeons perch precariously on the iron lattice, preening their blue and grey feathers. Their chivalry grows thin when they throw themselves collectively, in suicide fashion, as the 'Schools' safety valves explode their redundant fury. Flying low over the furrowed roof, their instant yet premature exit sweeps them to safer confines, to join hundreds of their greedy cousins scoffing the free spoil in Trafalgar Square.

The blushing signal anchored on its steel gantry at last repents and converts to bright green. As platform 5 is situated on the fireman's side, it is his responsibility to look to the rear and receive the guard's instruction for the right of way. But as expected, two or three late passengers are seen scurrying to reach the nearest carriage door. Seemingly unconcerned, the guard whistles his favourite tune, and the short sharp concord is as distinct as the green banner zig-zagging above his head. "Right Away Fred!" is my own verbal encore. The driver instinctively blasts the engine whistle that creates a double shrill, resounding throughout the station. Having now opened the regulator, the action mutes the roaring safety valves, they become as silent as the nearby Cenotaph occupying its place a stone's throw from Number Ten. With an awesome skirmish, a ten force gale discharges blatantly out of the open cylinder cocks. Their threatening behaviour manufactures an ominous blanket of steam that envelopes the steel latticed corridor to Hungerford Bridge. Hence, a quick and sudden closure isolates the cocks to reveal clear and normal visibility. An impulsive slip of the driving wheels compels the fire to dance with disgust, throwing waffles of black smoke skyward in quick retaliation, thus obscuring the elevated signal box, a nauseating "thank you" of boiling water for the signalmen's kind donation.

The 'Schools' were prone to slipping at the best of times because of their light weight, but Fred, reading the situation carefully, promptly closes the regulator and just as promptly opens it again, but this time the steam sanding gear is in full use. Finding her feet once again we slowly and deliberately trundle over Hungerford Bridge, with our eleven docile followers meekly surrendering to our every move. The now hollow and abrasive reception testifies audibly our suspension above the waters of 'Old Father' Thames.

The layout of track and rail points on the south side of the bridge, jolt us unkindly to find the main line into Waterloo station. Effectively, the exhaust beat rearranges a different tune as Fred modulates the gear lever to the desired percentage.

Looming visibly to our right, a picture postcard view of Westminster Bridge and the Houses of Parliament represent a tangible embodiment in front of a clear blue sky, and the serene waters express a natural blue haze, in stark contrast to our own vomiting volcano. The majestic clock unmistakably notifies a right time start, but Fred, fondling his own infallible time-piece, suspiciously examines both dials, and assures himself that his own faithful ticker must be the supreme commander!

Near and far, the pungent effluvium is strewn widely across the Thames, this black and white cloudscape, offensively arrests the immaculate buildings of Whitehall which house the world famous establishment of Scotland Yard, thus obscuring the passengers' picture postcard view!

At this early stage of the journey, the water injector is carefully put on. The action qualifies one simple, slow pull of the vertical handle above the boiler face. This operation automatically extracts water from the tender to feed the same into the engine boiler. When the injector was working, it was only then possible to activate the flexible engine hose principally used for dousing coal dust on both tender and footplate. A prudent spray was frequently encouraged for clean and comfortable working whilst on the running road.

Immediately prior to entering Waterloo station, the driver would habitually increase the engine blower before shutting off steam. This was necessary to elude the sudden surge of forced air tornadoeing up through the dampers and fire, to swallow the footplate complex with sheets of hungry flames emitting from the open firedoors. Over the years there have been scores of reports of enginemen being seriously burned for neglecting the steam blower. The blower was an effective instrument, for when operated it pulled the rush of primary air through the fire and boiler tubes to safely exit through the chimney. Some major reasons instrumental in causing these so-called 'blowbacks' were, for example, passing trains at close quarters, confined bridges and stations, and tunnels, which were the worst offenders.

The connecting side rods clank unrestrained into Waterloo, our noisy entrance is welcomed by one and all. Jubilant children holding bucket and spade fidget eagerly to be first aboard as Fred brings the train to a grinding halt. The collective bargaining for prospective seats is promptly sorted, while the romantics, looking for a place of solitude, have to settle for an abundant supply of unwelcomed chaperones. The now deserted platform reverberates the slamming of closing doors and the people disappear, but once again the guard's standing orders produces the usual sign language to permit *Clifton* to stutter to life. The driver's careful but emphatic manoeuvre prohibits the exhaust to lose its temper, and the powerful bluster throbs a coherent message acknowledged and gratefully received from the non-slipping driving wheels.

The bluish haze is a forewarning representing an urgent ultimatum that more coal be forthcoming, or else. The demanding entreaty is subsequently rewarded satisfactorily. A little over the front, and a few shovelfuls eased under the door duplicates an immediate response, for the frying coal puts forth a stinking black trail that sweeps every carriage roof with a flimsy touch, but the hanging congealment finds its own way, lingering formidably above the Blackfriars Road and over the congested traffic.

Although the water injector is still on, our steam pressure and water level are holding well as we charge full cry past Union Street sorting offices where they are busily composing Her Majesty's mail.

Our next green luminary opposite Ewer Street Continental sheds allows Fred to increase power to pull the brute weight over the slow curvature adjacent to the Cannon Street triangle. The oncoming commuter train is seemingly encroaching our road, but having implicit trust in the responsible signalmen, I convince myself it is not, and the contradiction becomes clearer as the train thunders by with only inches to spare.

With full boiler pressure and the gear lever back to the desired notch, our rear procession bends itself across the Borough High Street, centralising a formation to enter the confines of London Bridge number 4 platform. Our sharp whistle overtone preludes the thunderous entrance, and our physical wellbeing is greeted with jubilance from our standing spectators. Our accompaniment announces the keynote address, for the impertinent reveille from the tuneless safety valves discovers every orifice on the platform buildings, then bounces the earsplitting hullabaloo back over the footplate with a torturous quaver. Most passengers wisely stand clear, but their frightened toddlers cling for protection from their equally concerned loved ones.

Easing the blower and opening the firehole doors, the screaming white feather submits peacefully its full throated crescendo as the violent creature resigns at the signal gantry at the end of the platform. The water level is now bobbing in the top nut of the gauge glass, this of course represents a full boiler, so off goes the injector for the time being. The full boiler will now enable us to enjoy a good and consolidated start, so a cup of tea all round seems like a good idea, for the next part of the journey dictates no real let-up as far as Sole Street in Kent, with approximately 24 miles of fast and hard running.

In the meantime, the size of the firegrate deserves a mention, the 8ft 3in long grate provides an overall space of some 28 square feet. Quite a large stomach to feed! To master the skills of flashing the blade and placing the coal in a manner deserving best results, affords a considerable amount of time, especially left hand firing, as quite often a bilateral stance was required. My first encounter, as I humorously recall, was when graduating from Passed Cleaner to Fireman in 1955. All passed cleaners were required to travel as third man as part of the training programme, to feel the responsiblities of fast main line work, but under the watchful eye of a qualified main line fireman.

My own experience was a most embarrassing and upsetting occasion in more ways than one. I spent more long and humiliating periods cleaning coal off the footplate than depositing the same in the rightful place. For some unjustifiable reason, the firemouth had a continual habit of ruefully avoiding my swinging shovel, hence the mess on the footplate. Similarly, attempting to balance at 80mph on lurching floorboards was another tormenting feat in itself. The unimpressive postures fabricated an unusual but delightful "Charleston" and "Cha-Cha Jig" all rolled into one, with the firing shovel as dancing partner! It could have been a worthwhile audition with Victor Sylvester and his team of cabaret artistes.

Reverting back to the platform artistes at London Bridge, who were busily engaged in throwing goods and other paraphernalia to accompany the guard, they had now departed the scene, and once again the guard's tin whistle expressed the informative message. A positive glance sees him demonstrating his usual gestures exclaiming the 'off'.

Our own exquisite purge of high-fidelity, encouraged by a slight down grade pushes us away to a flying canter with no hint of protest.

Pushing fearlessly onwards, the front bogies overstate their responsibility, forcing the driving wheels to swing the motions in hot pursuit, their familiar jargon providing an auxiliary example for their loyal and supportive wheelstep followers. The pistons, pumping every revolution, sing their own independent song, sharing the publicity in launching the assault perfectly.

The cut-off, now fixed to the recommended percentage plus a wide regulator, causes the steam pressure to rise, a sure indication that the 'Schools' could be worked persistently at any level. Despite the maximum show of steam, a few more splashes of coal all round are necessary to maintain the present stature for the telling road to Sole Street. Not until we reach the Peek Freans biscuit works, approximately one mile hither, that a mandatory impulse conveyed the operation to work the water injector, not only to suffice the boiler level, but to hopefully stave off the threat of the white feather. It was considered a terrible waste of fuel and water if the engine was permitted to blow off steam. Although purposeful steps were taken to alleviate the pain, there were unavoidable situations that only enginemen can truly appreciate were beyond a certain control.

The fast and level stretch to New Cross permits our current speed to steadily improve, but because of a 50mph speed restriction, the driver eases the regulator down, knowing the present momentum will support the speed requirement swiftly to St John's with less deliberate effort.

Continuing along this elevated track from London Bridge, the road flows atop the original grey brick arches built in 1836. In 1850 and later in 1904, it was hitherto found necessary to widen this nearly four miles reach, to cope with the increased traffic demand. Surprisingly, the arched brick viaduct remains the longest in the world, as well as the Capital's oldest railway section, as I referred to in chapter three.

Navigating the route beyond the chocolate factory, our steady progress is exceptionally good, which must include, in my view, our rich external smokescreen. The full-flavoured condiment, festered with toxic filth swelled gloriously with an 'up' express reaching for Cannon Street, but without prior warning, another invisible odour attacks the train from all sides, and the strident intruder wrestles our own noxious stench. The warfare is short lived however, for our swift escape over Corbetts Lane bids farewell to the chocolate fumes to battle another day.

Aggressively thrashing New Cross station, our screaming whistle advocates not only the end of the speed restriction, but warns all passengers to stand well clear. Gathering momentum, the oscillation and bounce shows no compassion to the knuckles that turn a sickly white whilst hanging on for dear life.

With clear anticipation, the scenery now conveys a pensive mood, for the deepish cutting absorbs the train with a shadowy grip to be swallowed whole through the short sharp bridges like a scared snake angrily spitting smokey venom. Further, our impelling drive projects the green serpent triumphantly to emerge at St John's platform, with a pleasing end to the mile long encasement.

With somewhat dazzling but refined contrast, the compelling restitution in the shape of a hot heavenly jewel, offers a brilliant glow of encouragement, spreading an optimistic feeling throughout the train, securing a day of supreme bliss by the sea.

The signal at the end of St John's platform supports the proposed optimism, for it grants an injunction to continue our militant attack. Therefore, observing the green light, the driver shoulders the heavy regulator to full power, and being familiar with the hand-operated gear lever, winds the screw forward a couple of notches to execute an approved exhaust beat to cope with the imminent climb.

Cambering smoothly under the unshapely fly-over, the exhaust action is doubly clear as our speed now excells to sixty. This so-called *temporary* fly-over, hurriedly built with an oversized "Meccano Set" remains, in my opinion, a disgusting *thing,* an abominable memorial to those unfortunate passengers and guard who tragically perished there in December 1957. Moreover, I am convinced that the late Isambard Kingdom Brunel, the celebrated 'King of bridge construction', would have considered the *thing* as a humiliating joke, worthy of a good laugh. Shame on you British Rail. (A detailed account of the crash appears in chapter eight.)

At this stage of the trip, we can now afford to relax the water injector, for the boiler level is comfortably high, though the present thrust reduces the steam pressure, but no matter, such is the state of affairs that I am confident the white plumage will be tickling high at Grove Park, some three miles distant.

Moving congruently at a respectable pace, our eleven dependents sway and lean into the sharp right bend as the tale-telling blue haze from out of the chimney repeats another fierce reminder that I must contribute a renewed energy source to satisfy the incandescent glow.

The attacking haul also instructs approval to meet the energy demand for the continued strength.

In view of the foregoing, cautionary measures would need to be heeded when burning softer grade coal. For these reasons, self regulation and understanding summoned good judgement and timing of the highest degree, as overfeeding with slow burning coal destroyed combustion control with adverse results. By way of illustration, overeating will also refuse our own digestive system to consume our food intake appropriately in a balanced way, therefore, indigestion creates the ill effect. Therefore self-regulation, an acute understanding of our own personal needs obtains the best results for continued strength and energy.

Learning by one's mistakes, although perhaps pitiful at the time, can often create wholesome effects for the future, becoming a normal way for learning. This was true in getting to grips in understanding fully the effects of varied coal grades and to grasp firmly the administration of combustion control. Experience, coupled with a few mistakes, was the best teacher. Speaking for myself, I mistakenly concluded that if steam pressure dropped, this was the cue to heave shovelfuls of coal into the raging box, but not so, as I shamefully realised. Fruitful firing was not always manifested with the shovel, but a perfect example for success was retaining a sound knowledge of the permanent way. This foresight determined quite definitely a first class anticipation of knowing exactly when and how much coal and water were needed at any one time. Moreover, the precise genetics can only be augmented by firing practice. To complete the picture, I am sure our current safari will complement the techniques in practical terms.

Returning to the footplate, the measured throbs on the exhaust play a classical retreat to the waving signalmen at Parks Bridge Junction. Generally speaking however, signalmen and drivers were the best of friends, for they had to rely a great deal on one another, so a warm greeting was gratefully acknowledged on passing.

Our 400 ton haul presents no variation in rapidity, but the 'Schools' full-hearted effort presents an urgent referendum to quickly operate the water injector. Pounding over Lewisham High Street, the boiler supply is effectively rehearsed. The steam pressure preserves a healthy mark too, for the gauge needle is now trembling to overstep the maximum allowed. Simultaneously, the equally agitated safety valves wonder whether or not to let go their extreme velocity.

In an atmosphere of reeking steam, smoke and oil, the heat, both outside and inside, persuade the sweat glands to excrete profusely. Sharing the same perspiration, my clinging attire absorbs the discomfort like a wet sponge.

The engine's vibrating sequel subsides the coal to the shovelling tray that deliberately arranges a dust cloud as we charge the proximity of Hither Green number 4 platform. The train's external shock waves forewarn glad tidings of great joy, for my own three long and distinct engine whistles broadcast my confidential communiqué to my newly wedded wife of three months. The triple serenade (unknown of course to all) was happily received in the nearby terraced house in Theodore Road, and was knowingly interpreted to those "three little words". On through Hither Green station, the anticipated display of semaphore signals takes on a new dimension, expressing the end to the colour light signals through London.

Having now made a respectable run, our acceleration is observed thundering by Hither Green loco shed and the extensive goods sidings to our left. The expected hive of activity is a striking contrast to the soundless acres of thousands of grave stones reminding us of man's eventual destiny.

Although you would never know it, the motive power depot was a comparatively modern affair costing around £100,000 to construct in the early 1930s. The depot handled a majority of freight traffic, so the main locomotive complement consisted of freight engines. Sadly, as far as steam enthusiasts were concerned, by 1961 modern technology took firm control replacing steam with diesel locomotion.

Whilst adopting the firing once again, one was consciously aware how the power of the 'Schools', although under extreme stress, had complete mastery over the train. The evidence manifested itself as the speed intensified admirably under the footbridge at Grove Park, which separated London from Kent. The belching pour of swarthy spume smothered excited youngsters purposefully waiting for the foaming smog to ascend over the footbridge.

Just before entering the black hole of Chislehurst Tunnel, a new diesel-electric train (demu) bound for Hastings shows off its speed. Hurtling along on the 'down' main line, the driver, in collar and tie, sits smiling in his comfortable cab. Our galloping course invites further muscular activity to suffice the ravenous gourmet. One long whistle and short pip broadly advertises our dark encounter, informing any permanent way staff who might be working inside the tunnel, that our presence was nigh. Providing the steam pressure was comfortably high, I opened the fire doors, not only to decorate a glow of consolation, but also to subscribe a preliminary profit that reflected light to certify the water level and to check gauge readings etc. The half mile of black murk is over in seconds, but no sooner is the engine out of the tunnel than we swoop headlong through Elmstead Woods station that surrounds us with a beautiful tree clad cutting, now the Hastings train is just a square dot in the distance.

The left semaphore signal at Chislehurst Junction orders an easterly direction, plus 14 miles of undulating road to the summit of Sole Street. Now, for the first time, green fields cater an encompassment of an arranged and relaxed Kent environment, at least to Rochester. The distant signal at St Mary Cray strengthens our speed to seventy. Then at Swanley we rupture the eighty barrier with ease, for the road quickly descends to Farningham Road.

The clear but displeasing vibration shakes every nut and bolt on the footplate as well as every bone in the body, similar to a ride at the Canadian Bronc Riding Stampede in Calgary. The sheer and traumatic upheaval forces the knees to flex to ride out the charge of the 110 ton iron beast.

Through the dip at Farningham Road, the driver now supplements the steam chest to climb the impending bank. The impetus encourages the sudden grab to launch the train into the rise as the exhaust discovers its new ritual. A few spoons of coal advertises the 'Schools' energetic display with an enormous black look. Arrival at Meopham is a sure indication that only two miles remain to Sole Street summit. The hard slog slowly and surely take effect. Although we still require a full head of steam, we can close off the water injector and leave the shovel in the firing tray, for this stage affords opportunity to allow the water to come down in the boiler to counteract the steam pressure whilst descending the five mile bank into Rochester. This discernment provides a typical example of the aforesaid anticipation of self-regulation that comes with having an accurate knowledge of the running road. Thereby a great deal of coal and water can be saved.

Our speed on reaching Sole Street is approximately 50mph, but the start down the bank soon boosts the impelling force rapidly above seventy, so with steam shut off and the injector on, we are at liberty to relax and enjoy the green and pleasant land. The free coasting also lends us freedom to punish the stewed remnants in the teacan.

The cruel jostling and lurching is once again encouraged by the train's excelling motivation. The steel flap between engine and tender lifts and bangs defiantly with no let-up as train pushes engine down the 1 in 100 bank. Nevertheless, with a respectful yet buoyant, fear, one must anchor support in the driver's own confidence. It was difficult to expect a driver to have thoughts far removed from controlling an engine, especially at high speed. For the lives of passengers were the perishable goods in which they dealt. Therefore, in spite of the massive power at his fingertips, the first overriding conception must be the need to be consciously aware of the severity of the descent, knowing that in a few minutes our current 90mph dash may terminate ungraciously in the River Medway at the foot of the bank near Rochester, (the city where Charles Dickens once lived and wrote his last novel, *The Mystery of Edwin Drood*). A fine accomplishment indeed.

For their part, the biggest accomplishment has been enjoyed by the passengers, knowing they have progressed nearly halfway to the seaside. Despite their having an involuntary credulity in the crew, their own integral thoughts and intentions must understandably occupy first place in assimilating their own present day's activities. Meanwhile, our fast hurtle invites the distant motorway (M2), then under construction, to loom ever nearer, but the driver's thoughts and intentions are occupied for a different purpose. The forthcoming permanent speed restriction carries weight to his right hand, and his own involuntary assimilation reaches for the brake handle. An abstract preposition positively says "I don't fancy the idea of meeting the silent multitude peacefully resting in Rochester cemetery" Five to ten inches of brake is therefore necessary on the approach to Cuxton Road box. One needle on the brake gauge thankfully responds to the driver's touch, and the powerful inertia indulges the sonorous soundtrack as steel shoe and steel tyre rub shoulders with each other. The abrupt fight against the forces of gravity hide the water level in the top nut of the gauge glass, but only to expose itself again as the electrifying drag redresses the balance.

A passing 'up' train, punching distastefully against the ascent, shows off its own dynamic energy, holding the ground before it. For this reason, the heavy handed smoke-cloud slowly explores the green pasturage with every sort of tree it finds, and the fireman, maybe wishes that Isaac Newton had never been born, but from far off, the smell of battle lingers on.

Our slower approach at Cuxton Road stabilises the plunge to fifty on the advance to the bridges over Strood. Another splash on the brake checks the speed to thirty to take the 90° bend before trundling over the River Medway to enter Rochester station. On through the platform the driver introduces sufficient power to haul the long tailback into the short tunnel that serves as a portal to the imprisoned Chatham station, our first stop. The eastern end of the platform is no place to spend a summer day, being encased with bridges and tunnels, it gives a chilled atmosphere that can only be compared to the morgue inside the local hospital.

Stopping the engine under the solid brick arch, pinpoints an exact mooring to swing the water crane over the tender to replenish our water supply. Although it was not vital to do so, I cannot recall any occasion in my own experience where water was not obtained at Chatham. Perhaps for many drivers, it worked psychologically that repelled any worry as far as water was concerned, but making good use of the time, afforded opportunity to pull the coal forward to supplement what had so far been used.

The semaphore signal, rooted firmly at the other end of the bridge raises its arm and summons *Clifton* to proceed. Similarly, the steam pressure needle, now flirting the red line, authorises the courting plumage to raise the roof of the high bridge. The arched brickwork defiantly pushes the steamy dialogue from whence it came, with a voice which makes it thunder.

Sighting the green flag to our rear, the guard's mannerisms declare the 'off' and *Clifton* obeys, starting easily away into the tunnel just 50 yards ahead with no misgivings. The stiff climb to Gillingham commands the firing shovel to act swiftly, as the resonant cry from the explosive exhaust alters the frequency on the dark-side of the half-moon tunnel.

The feeling of such power moving under our instruction is great indeed, and gives one a serious sense of responsibility. The long blow on the whistle fractures the gloom and the torrid and intense atmosphere claims its authority under the earth, enveloping the complete train. Every passenger is affected in an indirect or personal way, for their nostrils and eardrums possess peculiarities far beyond those responsible in providing the discriminating sound and smell inside the tunnel.

No doubt chapter six will give you some idea of the remarkable originality displayed in the design of the 'Schools' class locomotive, how their prestigious faculties generate outstanding performances and, at their best, the class was brilliant in hauling over 500 tons. The 'Schools' current show through the two tunnels to Gillingham, in spite of the hard climb is supreme indeed, and must be considered equally favourable to other performances recorded in some contemporary railway publications that I have read.

On past Gillingham, despite our enthusiastic approach, the loco shed to the right has now lost its splendour. Not knowing which way to turn, the 50ft turntable has been pushed round by the Kent Coast Electrification Project that sparked into action in 1958. The significant feature conducted a new shape and motion to the railway industry, providing a sound and financial economic objective which has been firmly laid by the introduction of a parallel third rail, a steel fabric of railway policy, in the truest sense of the word.

Our rapturous exclamation over the level crossing does not explain the wind of change, but only the reason why traffic is halted either side of the white wooden gates. Charging along like troops in a battle, our performance is well demonstrated and beautifully held for another 18 miles to Faversham. Robert Louis Stevenson, the renowned English poet, seemingly believed in fairies and witches, but apart from that, he was no doubt a fast railway traveller. Mr Stevenson has a lot to say in his poem: *From a Railway Carriage* that may epitomize our sprint to Faversham. For the beautiful and mellow countryside of orchards and meadows, horses and cattle, mills and rivers and other naturalised activities of man, provides colourful and gentle reminder of the poet's visual expressions. Incredibly, his observations make no mention whatever of the glorious sight of smoke and steam, maybe the wind was blowing in a nonuniform direction, or maybe he just simply hated the sight of the stuff!

Tacking back to the footplate provides ample evidence to influence the passengers that our fast progress is now well established. Hence, our scream under the painted footbridge at Teynham beholds another five miles to Faversham. Faversham is an important junction that supports spacious goods sidings as well as a loco shed. The motive power depot worked in close relation with the Gillingham depot, and very often interchanged locomotives to suit their own working purposes. Subsequently, because of the Kent Coast Electrification Project, steam was completely withdrawn in 1959 and the shed buildings were converted to maintain and service diesel locomotives. The buildings still exist today in a derelict condition although with listed building status and can be seen clearly from the old iron footbridge that also still spans the complete railway complex. Furthermore, two primary routes remain the same. The shortest takes a south easterly direction via Selling and the cathedral city of Canterbury and then onwards to the White Cliffs of Dover. The presentation on this course portrays a landscape of lush green acres of hopfields and fruit orchards that explain why Kent is recognised famously as the 'Garden of England'.

By far the longest route hugs the north eastern coast which serves every seaside resort to Folkestone via Ramsgate. Our departure from Faversham pursues this latter route. The next seven miles to Whitstable meets with some rather sparse and flat marshland (Graveney), a complete contrast to the Canterbury route. Invariably, the flat and vacant estate projects a strong glare that refracts the sun's velocity and inundates the whole terrain, for the hypnotic influence produces a weird uninhabited spectacle. This straight stretch allows our speed to climb to seventy, and the salty breeze off the sea filters the exhaust fumes further inland to break the manifestation.

On this final stage of our safari, it is now necessary to measure the fuel relations, for all stations to Ramsgate are short hops and skips. Therefore, the steam negotiations over the productivity agreement must submit proposals for us to carefully manipulate our present state of affairs.

As we reach Whitstable, the town most famous for its oysters, the built-up area is most welcome, and the station clock outside the ladies' room suggests our timing as just about perfect. Within a couple of minutes we are off to tackle the stiff ascent to Herne Bay, but before we can say "Whitstable oysters", we pass under the overline bridge believed to be the oldest railway bridge in the world. (Today the bridge is no longer there, but one flank wall remains as a reminder of those early days.)

It was surprising to learn, especially in this remote part of the country, that this former six mile, single track line to Canterbury should have appeared as early as 1830. It was Mr William James, a solicitor and railway enthusiast, who saw the possibility of a railway line from Canterbury to Whitstable. It was a venture with all the right ingredients, for it was George Stephenson himself who was appointed to look after the project. The actual construction was contracted to Joseph Locke and John Dixon. However, the work involved cuttings and embankments, as well as a tunnel, nearly half a mile long through Tyler Hill. The principal reason for the rail link was, that it was hoped to reduce long and expensive road transportation, for the River Stour that was at one time used to carry merchandise, was no longer suitable because of heavy silt, and it was estimated would cost more than £80,000 to correct the problem. Whereby, Stephenson quoted a figure of £31,000 for the rail route which had the advantages of a direct course and obvious speed. After the completion, the first steam locomotive (*Invicta*) was introduced in Kent, and was subsequently delivered by the North Sea route from Robert Stephenson's factory in Newcastle upon Tyne.

Our present steam course from Herne Bay, Birchington and Westgate to Margate, is an almost unbroken chain of hotels, guest houses and a mixed bag of residential establishments with entertainment facilities and the like. Margate seemed to be the most popular resort on this north east coast. The majority of passengers who swelled the platform proved that fact significantly. Dreamland, a funfare for all ages, was perhaps the most pretentious attraction, but then the pier and sandy beach was only yards across the road from the station.

Starting away again, the steep up gradient excites the firing shovel, for once more coal is hastily sacrificed to the fiery furnace. Our excelling course inland opens into an agricultural province, apart from a few scattered houses and gentle roads, the habitation is as populated as our near empty train.

As we reach Broadstairs, Fred 'drops anchor' under the starter signal that points diagonally skyward like a breached shot gun. Overlooking the station is the familiar waterworks tower advertising itself as an ancient relic, no doubt for T.R. Crampton who designed the object with great expectations in 1859. Outside, along the narrow streets and overlooking Viking Bay is Bleak House where Charles Dickens wrote another of his famous books, *David Copperfield*.

We press on again at a firm pace, but not quite as fast as the greyhounds at Dumpton Park race track. Halting our gallant steed at Dumpton Park station, the meagre and somewhat unprofitable atmosphere is strange indeed, as lifeless as the planets in outer space, and it still remains so to this day.

The next important step for us at this stage, is not to gamble too heavily on the coal and water. Therefore, discipline now has to be more strict to avoid such a big fire. So sensible discernment and good judgement is the order, for the fire has to be cleaned at Ramsgate depot.

Up the steep bank and over the rise the hospitable Ramsgate station is invitingly clear. The station was built by A.W. Szlimper in 1926 in the same grey brick as Margate station that was also built in the same period. Although both stations are plainly built with the 1920's familiar stone masonry, Margate reveals a more robust character. It would appear that Hastings station (mentioned in chapter six) was also built on similar designs too – perhaps J.R. Scott pinched a few ideas at Margate.

While we wait for the shunter to uncouple the engine, we have an opportunity to wash our hands and face in the bucket of hot water I prepared up the bank from Dumpton Park, before we run light engine to the depot. Ramsgate depot was opened in 1930 with a complement of about 40 engines, which included a number of 'Schools'. Inevitably, because of man's aspiration to progression, Ramsgate depot was completely closed in December 1960; but most of the shed buildings remain in use, used for berthing electric trains.

While our relief crew attend to *Clifton's* refreshment, perhaps we can retreat to the crew mess room for a well-earned rest and cheese sandwiches before returning to London via the White Cliffs of Dover, in the next chapter.

5
Bulleid . . . and a 'West Country' Sprint in Kent

Throughout the years of steam, and up to the Second World War, there were many controversial practicalities of engine design and performance. Whatever their strengths and weaknesses however, they served their purpose well, and naturally the praiseworthy contributions from the men on the footplate adjudicated their machines as the finest in the business.

From the Second World War and onward, in fact right through to the end of steam traction, a new production of steam locomotive appeared. It was not only different in conventional design, but also differed considerably in every other way. Although unusual, this sleek yet unique looking locomotive transcended the Southern scene, and thus became the most elaborate engine ever developed up to that time. At this juncture therefore, let me explain briefly the revolutionary make-up and their splendid behaviour before we ride the footplate from Ramsgate to London (Victoria) via the famous White Cliffs of Dover.

Back in 1937, O.V.S. Bulleid, an ex-LNER man, took over as Chief Mechanical Engineer from Mr R.E.L. Maunsell who retired from the position in the same year. Bulleid manifested himself as a master engineering genius in his own right. He was a man dedicated to justify his own ideals and recommendations as far as engine performance was concerned. Without doubt he learnt a lot from his former colleagues and past contemporaries. In fact his previous post at the LNER was second-in-command to Sir Nigel Gresley, the originator of the renowned A4 class Pacifics of which *Mallard* still holds the official world speed record for the steam traction of 126mph.

Apart from modifying engines, Bulleid presented himself well in the eyes of the railway world. His impressive tone introduced no less than four new productions for the Southern Railway. Their designations are as follows: First, the Q1 class 0-6-0, or the "Ugly Duckling" as it was called. Secondly, the 'Merchant Navy' class 4-6-2, an impressive green monster, with a power to match. Thirdly, the 'West Country' and 'Battle of Britain' classes of 4-6-2, which were both the very same design, the only difference being their name assignment. Fourthly, the ambiguous 'Leader' class the last of Bulleid's productions. Their ordinary, plain appearance was more like a windowless London tube carriage than a proposed steam engine. They were disappointing to say the least and only five were assembled and not all completed. Later, in 1951, record has it that they were quietly scrapped.

Without having to recall specific examples here, not all of Bulleid's originalities seemed clear-cut. He discussed many disputes at length, airing the arguments on both sides and offering solutions accordingly. No matter how weighty the tradition or argumentation, his judgement was a decisive one, whereupon his new enterprise was given the seal of approval, proposing a confidence of the highest calibre.

In particular, it was Bulleid who designed the first British all-welded boiler, saving an influential amount of weight by side-stepping the use of rivets, as well as additional metal which was heavily consumed in lap joints. Thereafter, the stately and evocative 'Merchant Navy' class was launched from Eastleigh Works in 1941. With this, Bulleid employed his new overtones to the full, the result being an extremely powerful green giant producing a tractive effort of some 37,500lb.

Not quite original, but naturally acceptable, must surely have been the enclosed cab with sliding windows. The whole cab section married smoothly into the tender. No more worries of running tender-first, exposed to appalling weather conditions, as experienced in chapter three. For its part, the new so-called 'air-smoothed' casing covered everything but the wheels and side motions. A curious rectangular box mounted on twelve wheels, or a "Spam Can" as they were traditionally dubbed, without the key. Even the wheels were different, a perforated air smoothed type instead of the original spoked type.

Comparing the new 'Merchant Navy' Pacific with the older A4 Pacifics, one can clearly see a tinge of Gresley's personality as opposed to the external casing and enclosed cab on Bulleid's engine. But one original invention we cannot deny Bulleid, was the valve gear. All three cylinders were activated by a hefty chain interacted from the middle axle, The steel chain and driving mechanism, being completely immersed in an oil-bath, saved the driver both time and the uncomfortable bother of oiling up the centre motion. The depot fitters themselves were responsible for changing the oil, and top-up procedures.

Despite the war however, on 22nd February 1941, a trial run was carried out. The new locomotive performed with supreme authority, pulling 20 bogies (coaches) from Eastleigh to Bournemouth and back. Well satisfied with the merchandise, a ceremony was officially held at Eastleigh two weeks later to name the green prototype (No. 21C1) *Channel Packet*.

The smooth, quiet running, was far superior to existing locomotives. Truly a "Rolls-Royce" amongst steam engines. The boiler was an exceptionally good steam producer, no doubt the unique Nicholson thermic syphons were instrumental in this. These took the shape of two large six inch diameter curved tubes which were fixed from the tubeplate and tied into the firebox crownplate, positioned above the furnace. Consequently, the direct temperature influenced the water content to superheat, and thus appropriately circulate in compliance with the heat rising principle.

The two fire-hole doors were a heavy steam-operated affair, and a foot-pedal inspired the half-moon wings to open sideways and up, and subsequently close with a solid hammer-to-anvil strike. Like most other firemen, I could not get on with them. It was far simpler, and more straight-forward to hand operate the clumsy apparatus. Although, as far as I can recall (in the 1950s), much of the equipment never worked, and was thus discarded. Perhaps that was one good reason why the idea was scrapped on the later and rebuilt models.

The firebox, unlike the conventional long and narrow construction, was almost square, about seven feet by six. The fireman concentrated exclusively on heaving the coal round the back corners and under the fire door. This action required placing the shovel blade completely in the maw of the raging fire and then bringing it smartly back. A roll of both wrists emptied the coal into the desired spot. Their appetite was "greedy", to be kind. Anything not much less than one and a half tons was judged a satisfying box full. As long as the fuel was alight, this reinforced a good start before any trip, but thereafter, the engine was not too keen on scoffing between meals, perhaps odd shovelfuls of purpose-placed coal 'round the back corners' and a little over the front, pacified her desire, using the 'little but often' principle. That practice was determined according to the weight being hauled, and knowledge of the route ahead, where experience was the prevailing denominator.

One could rest assured that under normal circumstances, I hasten to add, despite any kind of arduous toil, a Bulleid Pacific steam pressure needle literally 'trembled' between the 250 and the 280 maximised mark with little, if any, deviation. I cannot recall on any occasion having difficulties maintaining steam, such was their remarkable elaboration. Their only fault, from the driver's point of view was perhaps, that smoke and steam exhaust had occasion to billow and roll back out of the chimney above the flat boiler top to obscure the narrow windows and blinding the road ahead. Although intrusive at times, it became an accepted nuisance which, contrary to certain published opinions I have read, did not really cause too much trouble for most drivers.

Another most excellent advantage, from the fireman's point of view this time, was the electric destination lights fitted both front and rear. Even the cab, gauge glasses and steam reverser had their own independent electric light, home from home comfort beyond compare. All that was missing, was a fitted carpet, two fire-side chairs, and music to gently filter the ears. A generator slung under the cab provided the required power supply. In keeping with statutory regulations, a paraffin tail lamp had still to be secured to the engine rear when running light. This conformity notified train completeness, but at most, the fireman kept three oil lamps trimmed and filled in case of emergency.

Additionally, this super express passenger engine was now commissioned to head the impressive "Golden Arrow" boat train from London to Dover, commencing again in October 1946. Understandably, this famous train had been suspended during the period of the war. Prior to the war, in fact for 15 years from 1924, a Maunsell 'King Arthur' class 4-6-0 locomotive was the regular assignment to speed the posh and luxurious train to and from Dover, non-stop, inside a measured time of 1 hour and 45 minutes. On few occasions however, a 'Lord Nelson' headed the distinguished train. The all Pullman carriages, in their famous cream and chocolate livery, departed Victoria at 10.50am and arrived at Dover Marine at 12.32pm. Just for the record, this unique and appropriately named "Golden Arrow" was not officially adopted as such until May 1929.

Immediately after the war, Bulleid's 'West Country' and 'Battle of Britain' classes contended the scene. Their appearance was similar in every way to the 'Merchant Navy' class. The only *real* difference was their maximum axle load of $18^{1}/4$ tons as compared with 21 tons of the 'Merchant Navy'. The cylinders too were slightly reduced, 16¾in as against 18in on the MN, but overall, they were purposely scaled down to rid weight in order to venture territories where the nine ton heavier counterpart was restricted.

One other significant change was the fire-grate, as a drop section was neatly installed. This introduction saved the fireman having to heave cwts of ash and clinker out through the fire door, across the footplate and onto the track-side. Instead, all clinker etc, was methodically dropped through the grate and ashpan to fall into the pit below, thus avoiding dust and clinker droppings which sometimes branded the wooden footplate boards.

The name 'West Country' really speaks for itself. Each individual engine was bestowed with names of the English west country towns of Devon, Cornwall, Somerset, Dorset and Wiltshire. Names such as *Exeter, Plymouth, Launceston, Salisbury, Yeovil* and *Bodmin* were just six priority choices. For the 'Battle of Britain' locomotives, or BoBs as they were traditionally dubbed, it was decided to name each after Royal Air Force squadrons, or names applicable thereto, for example: *Biggin Hill, Manston* and *Spitfire*. Even Winston Churchill, the war-time premier, had his name attributed on No. 34051. A coat of arms was also emblazoned underneath the engine name, or given title. The whole idea was for the nationalistic purpose of commemorating the defeat of the German Luftwaffe over the counties of South East England. However, in view of the foregoing Bulleid productions, a complete list of names and appropriate numbers is appended to the end of this chapter.

As late as 1958, many of the 'West Country' locomotives were completely rebuilt and modernised to transpose some of the drawbacks manifested in the older engine. For example, the chain-driven apparatus exposed malfunctory symptoms, whereby the enclosed sump system proved impractical and very costly, as far as repair and maintenance was concerned. The new converted models were fitted out with three sets of Walschaerts valve gear, thus providing easy access all round. The steam reverser had its heartaches too. The lever habitually crept unnoticed, allegedly caused by a fault in design as well as vibration when running. Thus, to keep still the wandering pointer, a new type of lever was favoured, and included an easier sighted drum indicator which locked the percentage thereon.

Gone too was the unwieldy steam equipment which opened and closed the fire doors. A manual device, no different from the old type, remained a simple one lever movement.

The external 'air smoothed' casing was no longer featured either. The finished article, as the illustrations show, was more like a traditional steam engine by far. As regards the aforesaid 'rolling smoke' problem, I can honestly say the new improved shape made no improvement whatsoever. It was my own personal experience that smoke and steam still rolled back over the cab windows, inhibiting forward visibility.

The only other inclusion, for the purpose of safety, was the new engine was installed with a 'hot bearing censor'. This meant, if the middle big-end overheated, due to lack of oil, a strong whiff of garlic penetrated the footplate as a warning message which hopefully disturbed the mental powers of the driver's brain. It was my belief, according to discussions on the subject, that most Bricklayers Arms drivers were not too sure what garlic looked like, let alone what it smelt like! Perhaps an odour of rotten eggs might have been more acceptable.

Having now given you a condensed synopsis of Bulleid's Pacifics, let us now board the footplate of a rebuilt 'West Country' class No. 34012 *Launceston* to begin an adventurous and sparkling sprint to Victoria. Our train, standing in Ramsgate station, consists of ten red and cream Bulleid corridor coaches which form an extra afternoon special, let's say the 5.15. The immaculate 'West Country' is as new and crisp as fresh baked bread direct from the Eastleigh ovens. In complete contrast and reminiscent of bygone years, is the gas lighting still in use on the station platforms. Interestingly too, the electrification conductor rails are newly positioned, and preside as long steel misfits, awaiting their call for duty. Therefore, the year of our journey would have to be 1958.

Alas! On this occasion, I cannot recall the name of the young driver for whom I was firing. It could have been several drivers, but four possible candidates spring readily to mind as follows: Bill Dodson, or was it Dobson?, Harry Bishop, Sid Earl or maybe Percy Collier. My "out of the hat choice" fell to the latter because of my uncertainty, therefore I will nominate Percy Collier as driver on the forthcoming trip.

Launceston's enclosed cab motivates a tropical atmosphere ideally suited for wintry conditions, but on this occasion, winter is a long way off. Although, considering the sun was low in the sky, the weather was warm, even Percy takes his jacket off.

Placing the full tea-can on the mantle-tray, I examine the fire. It is well alight and equally established high up to the fire-hole doors. Positioning the shovel blade inside the furnace, I carefully tunnel air to the front of the fire just below the brickarch. This customary practice discloses probable deficiences or areas where the fire is either too thick or too thin. Satisfied with the existing content, I work the water injector to prevent a dramatic outburst from the safety valves, which may cause the Station Master to speak rapidly in a non-temperate language.

Unlike the older models, the new 'West Country' boiler is only pressed at 250 psi, but I do not think the reduction has made a scrap of difference to the engine's strapping personality.

Having observed the guard's signal, I take delight in pulling the whistle cord. A few more than interested spectators stand on the platform watching our every move. At last we are off, exactly on time. The regulator wide open, *Launceston* accelerates noticeably away with great vigour, and thankfully the driver notches the gear lever progressively back. Shutting the injector off, I sit down, leaning my head out of the side window and hold my cap on at the same time. The somewhat rapid and wolfy exhaust pushes out grey and white clouds over towards St Lawrence's church. Our speed quickly increases under the low road bridge greeting the sparse countryside with a disturbing throng. The yonder flat and silver sea glistens ominously, but arches itself peacefully in Pegwell Bay where, once upon a time, the Vikings landed their long-boats. Only the far-off power station and its massive cooling towers spoil the flat and natural beauty.

As anticipated on this route, a permanent way check east of Minster entices the safety valves to blow-off angrily. Whilst I put the injector back on, the 'distant' semaphore signal tells Percy to wrench the steel throttle forward once again. Then, the valves quietly sit down overlooking the exhaust trail above and beyond the River Stour.

Our journey for the ongoing twelve miles to Deal is fairly easy going, presenting no great problems, but afterwards, a 1 in 100 upward climb to Martin Mill, an eight mile stretch, will present our first real challenge.

However, for someone without practical experience of a steam locomotive, I must add that the power source is not simply there 'on tap'. Unlike electric and diesel power, which has power there for the asking, the fireman has to *manufacture* it according to immediate demand, while the driver uses it to his topmost advantage.

Two miles before Deal I begin my own manufacturing proceedings. It is surprising how much fire, particularly round the back corners, has been whittled away by the exhaust suction, truly living up to its greedy reputation. Therefore, with heaped shovelfuls under the door and back corners, three or four lighter shovels down each side and front corners, put back that which has been lost. Slamming the 'butterfly' doors shut with a resounding thwack, black smoke thickly departs inland, sedating furthermost fields towards Canterbury.

I note the pressure needle quivering nicely on 250 as we pass the small station of Deal, but Percy increases power for the impending off-shore ascent. I next shut off the injector, for the boiler level is remarkably high in the glass. I place a few more shovelfuls under the door for good measure, but leave the wing doors open one notch, knowing that will suffice until Dover Priory.

We gallop on at about 50mph earthquaking the small wooden signal box at the end of Walmer station, perhaps spilling the signalman's tea. Such is the engine's performance, we climb effortlessly up the bank, portraying an overture between a working sewing machine and an escaped 'swag-man', hardly believing we are hauling ten heavy coaches full of human bullion.

Another permanent way check at Martin Mill causes the driver to close-in the regulator, and so I am influenced to work the injector yet again. Black smoke immediately pours over the station buildings, defiling the slate roof and processing a rich pong for station staff and the like; absolutely wonderful from my point of view! I thus reluctantly opened the fire doors to help rid the black fog, and we both celebrate with a cup of hot tea.

Despite our free coasting, the speed strengthens on the descent, and the white radiation and incandescent glow light up every cranny on the footplate, drawing sweat down my face. The blower half on stops any chance of a blow-back as another steam train whistles by, heading for Ramsgate, extracting a second portion of black death for Martin Mill staff.

A small steam flurry flutters above the safety valves as Percy eases down the brass brake handle, subsequently slowing us rapidly to 20mph. Receiving the all-clear yellow "Fishtale" (semaphore distant signal), the driver yanks open the regulator with just enough steam in the chest to support momentum. It is no surprise, that the remarkable originality displayed by *Launceston* brings us quickly into the blackness of the short Guston Tunnel, and in seconds to emerge swiftly into the sharp bend just east of Kearnsey where the junction picks up the main north westerly line to London. The same route projects some of the best scenic acres of hop-vines and fruit orchards manicured in Kent, right through to Selling and Faversham. Approaching the junction, the sun has a habit of springing from one place to the next in quick succession. With our front end bathed gloriously in sunlight, further on, the complete right side of the train faces into the celestial glow. Finally, on the straight stretch past the junction, which incidentally, affords a grand spectacle of Dover Castle across a valley, the orange sphere disappears behind the train as we drift the last two miles to enter the short Priory Tunnel and the station immediately beyond. Such were the bends prior to Dover.

We arrive at the Priory six minutes down because of adverse signals. Confidently, Percy glances at his well-used watch and says: "We'll pull it back on the straight stretch between Ashford and Tonbridge . . . so keep the old kettle boilin' won't yer". With that we again enjoy another cup of stewed tea before tackling the forthcoming 78 miles to London Victoria.

On the railway, time was not only crucial and morally strict, but more often than not, it was regarded as a railman's 'number one' enemy. Time had always the upper-hand creating an attitude of contempt if not controlled. Therefore one strove to give or take at all legitimate cost, and it was the duty of everyone concerned, however torturous, to exercise every possible means to coordinate the best solution in recapturing it, if lost. So, providing the road ahead is clear, with no unhealty circumstances to contend with, there is no reason why our current time loss cannot be recovered, particularly on the 30 mile level dash between Ashford and Tonbridge.

Percy looks out for the right-of-way while I quickly feed the fire with an economy diet of soft Kentish coal. Gratefully the blower pummells the smoke vertically above the station, but I cannot stop the screaming feather (safety valves) terrorising a gathered throng closeby. At this very moment we are off and the safety valves reduce their strength to a satisfying hiss.

Our next hop is a continuous twelve mile climb to Sandling Tunnel, but first we hug the famous white cliffs through Folkestone Warren. Passing Dover motive power depot to our left, *Launceston* picks up the thrown gauntlet and presses hastily onward towards Shakespeare Tunnel. Just before entry, I put the injector on, customary practice afore any long tunnel. At the same time, the driver reaches up to rehearse the whistle as we tear aggressively into the tunnel entrance. This somewhat unusual twin bore tunnel was cut through around the 1840s, initiated by Sir William Cubitt. The two Gothic style portals resemble Normandy architecture – narrow, yet tall and arch pointed. On the approach however, one wonders how on earth such a wide train can ever get through! Emerging safely at the other end (1,387 yards) is convincing proof that Mr Cubitt had got his sums right.

Looking back over the train, the carriages chase us out of the smoke-filled exit, but only to be entertained with a steep fortress of chalk cliffs dropping to the track-side. The left side embellishes a shallow fall, edging away to the sea, doing a far better job than King Canute. My voice bursts forth in song, a real extravaganza above the beat of the engine descant: "There'll be blue birrrds overrrr the white cliffs of Doverrr". Percy stares disapprovingly, knowing he would rather listen to the soothing voice of Vera Lynn.

Suddenly, everything goes dark, a whistle duet explains we have encountered the confines of Martello Tunnel, a conventional half-moon bore which offers greater breathing space. Finding daylight at the other end, we hammer fearlessly on to cross the yellow brick road atop the mighty Foord Viaduct which gently rolls us into Folkestone (Central) station, our next stop.

This colossal viaduct is worthy of mention, for it engorges a breathtaking sight which offers a transcendent view of the harbour and town centre. Similar to the Shakespeare Tunnel, this superlative building was another construction originated by Sir William Cubitt in the 1840s. Its tall, 100ft brick piers support 19 brick arches. The viaduct remains a fine spectacle to this present day, and well worth a closer look, that is if one appreciates engineering feats of 'high quality' and human ingenuity, far superior indeed to the magical arts in the "Land of Oz". Over the years the viaduct has undergone extensive repair works and looks more like a 'red' brick viaduct than the original 'yellow' brick.

With a whistle and a stutter we purge under the signal gantry adjacent to the signal box. The ongoing sprint will now continue inland for about 42 miles to Tonbridge, our next scheduled stop. For nearly six miles to Westenhanger, the road rises at an average of 1 in 280, no trouble whatsoever for No. 34012 and her ten immaculate followers. I splash a few shovelfuls of coal around as necessary as we gain momentum inside the short Sandling Tunnel. Reaching Smeeth, the speed rapidly grows to something like 60mph. Of course all speeds have to be estimated, for there is no indication provided on any of Bulleid's engines nor any other engines for that matter, although, the later BR Standard classes, as referred to in chapter eight were provided with such.

Opening her out, Percy gives the loco its head, and subsequently alters the cut-off accordingly. For the steam pressure, the needle shivers nicely on 240.

A mile or so south of Ashford, the firing shovel sees action once again, and, filling the back corners, I know that this will probably suffice until Tonbridge. Ploughing smoothly over merging roads from Canterbury and Hastings, *Launceston* purrs like an entranced 'moggy' chasing an invisible 80mph mouse under the bridge through Ashford, but at the same time, depositing a white blanket over the station. Inflicted with yellow pride, the 'distant' signal before the station has raised its arm skyward, recommending no speed reduction. Hanging onto the whistle we see passengers instinctively move back off the platform in an effort to escape the sudden barrage. Then, the driver examines his watch while I inspect the tea-can. My shrug and silent gesture tells Percy it has all gone. Scrutinising the gauge glass reminds me to give the boiler a drink instead. I then sit down to help spot forthcoming signals on the long and out-of-sight track.

After Ashford, the oncoming road enjoys a 30 mile straight line, culminating at Tonbridge. Our speed by now must have exceeded to above ninety to hopefully regain the lost time. Although difficult to judge, I reckon the speed passing Headcorn and Staplehurst stations must have topped the 100mph barrier. One could, quite literally, feel the rails lifting to meet the wheels, enforcing a firm and fast adhesion in their respective spring.

Of subservient interest, most engine men I am sure, took design and engineering skill much for granted, having no intelligible comprehension of the scientific principles accumulated between the wheels. A train travelling at high speed has capabilities perfectly timed and finely segmented according to mutual relativity. But the prestigious mathematical make-up of metals under stress, and the intrinsic dimensions of the stresses which occur, leaves a wealth of unknown knowledge beyond a driver's normal comprehension. That is why one can truly admire the works of Bulleid, Maunsell, Urie, Gresley and other mechanical engineers who worked out the genetic chemistry and scientific intricacies involved.

Recent history has confirmed that speed capabilities have propagated somewhat dramatically. We only have to think of the jet aircraft, the improved vitality of shipping, the refinery put into the internal combustion engine, not to mention hundreds of other contributory factors in the field of developing speed, to appreciate the vast potential already derived.

However, it is with the aforementioned facts in mind, plus a bit of human reasoning and logic, that the currently held world speed record for steam traction should have been broken long ago. If for example, Bulleid's 'Merchant Navy' class was offered equal opportunity, I am confident the 126mph steam record would therefore no longer stand. With all due respect, Gresley's *Mallard* (the present holder) will always remain, from my point of view at least, a questionable 'king of steam' speed, for the record was never challenged with later improved models. (Gresley's *Mallard*, along with a rebuilt 'Merchant Navy', No. 35029 *Ellerman Lines* are both preserved at the National Railway Museum, York).

During the time it has taken you to read the last three paragraphs, we now stride unperturbed amidst a stronghold of well established hop gardens and oast houses galore, a typical environment of Kent status.

With about 20% cut-off, and a modest strain of steam through the cylinders, No. 34012 spurs ever onwards through Paddock Wood, subscribing a speed faster than usual. With only six miles to Tonbridge remaining, the driver shuts off steam with no sense of speed loss. At length though, the speed eventually falls away to about fifty, but is assisted with a slight brake application. Opening wide the fire-hole doors, the congenial hue invites a closer look . But alas!, and as presumed, the fire has by now deteriorated substantially, although the steam pressure holds up all the way.

In anticipation of the forthcoming ascent to Knockholt (1 in 122), I recharge the firebox, finishing before reaching Tonbridge station. As fast as I can feed the half-starved monster, its voracious appetite consumes the coal beyond that which was normal, like a young starling gobbling 'grub' from its mother's beak.

Again I hear Percy splash the brake a touch to control the swing in to the left points at about 20mph. The abrupt lurch exclaims, that the leading bogie wheels have found the local line which runs parallel with the main central track, both lines sweeping progressively under individual arches below the High Street. Slowly we sidle affront the platform and stop further on, opposite the lone water column, where we take on water.

"Cor! would yer believe it! . . . we've only taken 20 minutes from Ashford and now only one minute down – not bad eh?" says Percy excitedly. By my own unofficial reckoning that was an average speed of some 90mph, and I must add, on not much more than half-power.

Surprisingly however, the guard comes up onto the footplate. 'What's 'e want?' I wonder. 'Not a chin-wag surely', I think, but he says: "Well done driver . . . ya' certainly made up time from Ashford. .. Yer must ave bin doin' 'undred". Then his words continued in a more sombre mood: "We've gota few young soldiers on board, apparently on leave, celebrating with a few bottles. I think they got on at Folkestone. It appears they've 'ad-a-bit too much t'drink, they've even smashed a toilet and damaged a seat. I've told the station master, and es gonna phone Victoria to get the railway police". After a few more choice words, Percy replies: "Righto chum" and with that the guard hurries off into the train.

"That lot should be court-martialled and shot the . . ." but no longer able to contain themselves, the safety valves also burst forth rudely, draining out Percy's further comment. "We might be shot if we don't scarper quick" I shout, with a false sense of concern, Percy just smiles, and the guard blows his whistle. After all that, we are now ten minutes behind schedule.

Like a boxer eager to begin his fight, I notice that Percy has every intention of making up the lost time again. Thus in so doing, No. 34012 scorches onward promoting the path of steel which leans agreeably into the keen right bend away from the continuous intersection from Redhill. Most passengers can now be seen clearly sitting in their seats, with no signs of war from the delinquent soldier boys.

The sun has long gone west and the scene encompasses rich and fertile fields betwixt the far-off twilight zone. Pulling enthusiastically over the River Medway, *Launceston* preserves her stamina well against the start of the ongoing twelve mile climb. For the first time since leaving Ramsgate, the steam pressure needle falls to 230 as the train straightens out for Hildenborough, but that is no reason for panic. Another inspection of "Dante's Inferno" causes me to spread a little more coal in defence to meet the oppressive threat.

Four miles on, we boldly enter the 'hell-hole' and slippery depths of Sevenoaks Tunnel, which stretches for nearly two miles (1m 1,693 yards) under the Greensand Ridge. Our speed on entry, against the gradient of course, must be about fifty, and even so, this is well above what is considered normal. With the injector singing, and the sanding gear moaning, we pursue the battle, knowing the conquest of time is paramount. In support, I shoot more coal to the greedy 'warlord', and the driver notches his lever forward a peg. With dignity and splendour, white cinders scatter off the tunnel roof, and a black veil enshrouds the train. As in the nature of true speculation, the gauge needle enthrones itself in association with the song of war, like a distinguished aristocrat, shivering commendably on 240lbs. Even the whistle joins in the rally for the third time.

Emerging from the underground cavern, the welcome daylight arouses the eyes to a new temperament of paradise. A few hundred yards on, amongst a forest of tall Edenic trees, *Launceston* grabs the 'bit' between her teeth and springs headlong through Sevenoaks station. Under the bridge we career, over the left 'Y' junction towards Dunton Green where the 1 in 143 ascent is less aggressive.

Displaying his watch, and a face alight with optimism, Percy bawls across the footplate "We're only five minutes down now chum". For a short duration, the road before Dunton Green converts down-hill to the station, by which the impulsive motivation lifts the train to Polhill at about 65mph. As is customary, I now have to think in terms of fire reduction, rather than fire production. For when we arrive at Victoria, the engine is subsequently destined to run light to Stewarts Lane depot for disposal purposes.

Our next encounter invades yet another abyssmal tomb, namely, Polhill Tunnel, a long cavern of 1m 851 yards. This tunnel however, composes the basement under the North Downs not far from the delightful Darent Valley. The fast inrush displaces a mixture of cold and stale air that miserably swirls the entrance, a physical process foreign to all but enginemen. Emerging from the tunnel, the speed has dropped to about 45mph, but then, the summit is now only yards ahead, spelling a welcome end to the uphill assault from Tonbridge. Developing speed over the summit, we now converge the short Chelsfield Tunnel. My own inventive sign language informs the driver, the yonder 'distant' signal, just prior to the tunnel, is raised high, clearing the road before us. A long scream on the whistle, and the train sweeps the right curve as smooth as an archer's bow driving headlong inside the dark hole. In seconds we shoot out as straight as an arrow aiming for Orpington. From now on, the route is fairly easy going, as far as firing is concerned, as we shall see.

A ten mile down-hill sprint to Penge, which incidentally, starts the outer skirts of South East and South West London. A complete and stark contrast to the plush gardens of Kent. The hard climb through Penge Tunnel (1m 381 yards long) literally ducks under the Crystal Palace where the once renowned glass structure was built, characterising the same name. It was however, Sir William Cubitt again who supervised the unique glass structure, for which he acquired his knighthood. Sadly it was destroyed by fire in 1936. The last sprint invites a few twists and turns over and through strategic and populated suburbs, to finally cross the River Thames and into Victoria station.

Infringing Orpington hospital, and a quick wave to the nurses, the gallant 'West Country' lunges through Orpington at something like 70mph. Here, the track immediately multiplies into four. The speed from now on, because of the digressional route ahead, is both varied and conditional, permitting only sixty and less, particularly on the Victoria line through the suburbs.

Orpington however, provides a country terminal for electric trains from both Charing Cross and Victoria, a suburban shuttle service to and from.

Another check to Percy's watch sees three minutes recovered. But then taboo, trepidation, and Calamity Jane! The diverging 'distant' signal north of Orpington is well and truly 'on'. "That's all we want" cries Percy, grabbing the brake handle at the same time. "Looks as if we're gonna stop at Petts Wood" he adds loudly, shaking his head in disgust. Sure enough, the red semaphore 'home' signal remains as horizontal as a dead door nail, shackled permanently to the signal post. The train itself rolls just as dead to a long and squeaky halt. Some passengers, including the guard, look out anxiously, wondering why we have stopped so abruptly.

At Percy's request, and in relation to railway policy of course, I proceed to the signal telephone and present our identity and destination. Briefly, the signalman explains the reason for our delay. Apparently, the communique relay system, from section to section, foretold our train for Charing Cross, yet the engine's front code boards display clearly a *Victoria* exhibit. The observant signalman at

Sevenoaks had noticed the contradiction, and therefore originated our present stoppage.

Misinterpretations of that sort occurred from time to time, but more often during busy summer seasons. What with 'extra' and 'special' excursions, signalmen were no doubt kept busy identifying respective trains. Perhaps the law of averages needed to be justified "somewhere along the line".

I recall one such occasion, a young Bricklayers Arms driver, who incidentally, will remain anonymous, carelessly took the wrong route and finished up at Victoria instead of Charing Cross. What happened was this. The signalman at Chislehust Junction, (just yards ahead from where *Launceston* is now standing) had received the oncoming train to be Victoria bound, thereby, setting the route forthwith. Approaching Chislehurst Junction from St Mary Cray, on the Chatham line, the B. Arms driver brought his passenger train into the junction. Unfortunately for him, he wrongly accepted the clear road left to Bickley and Bromley (the Victoria route). In fact, he should have been given the right semaphore for Elmstead Woods and Grove Park (the Charing Cross route). Although the signalman set the road incorrectly, he was, nevertheless, not to blame. He was after all, only obeying information received from the previous section. Therefore, the responsibility must rest squarely on the driver's shoulders. For it was he, and he alone, who verified knowing the road by signing for such. According to railway decree, all drivers after learning their routes, were required to confirm such knowledge by signature. Inevitably, disciplinary action thus ensued for the humiliated B. Arm's driver. Quite rightly, there was no excuse, as far as railway authority was concerned.

When confronted with a signal error, such as the aforesaid, the only and proper course open to the driver, is to sound the whistle three times on approach. This will inform the signalman that something is wrong. If not correctly adjusted immediately, then the fireman proceeds to the signal telephone.

You may now understand, from the aforesaid incident, and the geographical location, why it is that the signalman has no alternative but to stop 'our' train at Petts Wood, just prior to where both main lines to London diverge at Chislehurst.

Getting back to our own present incident, we find our train negotiating Bromley South station at about 60mph, with no real hope of restoring the lost time. The two miles straight descent from

Chislehurst, sweeps our 400 tons into a right curve before Shortlands and picks up the direct route to Victoria. (The longer route branches right from Shortlands via Catford and Crofton Park, usually saved for excursion traffic.)

A permanent way check distills any hope of a fast gallop through Beckenham. Advancing progressively at thirty, the safety valves adopt a deafening roar, terrorising Beckenham Junction station and a few passengers waiting in coloured dresses. Perusing the fire concludes that it should be sufficient for Victoria thus far. Grasping the short rake, I push the fire content all over the grate, knowing the climb inside Penge Tunnel would contribute aggressively, and rid excess fire to an even spread.

Injector now on, the driver opens the regulator wide at Kent House, the end of the speed restriction. The 'West Country' charges like a mad bull after a toreador up the present ascent. Our effort becomes more apparent when *Launceston* rudely awakens the privacy of Penge East station. The vibrant and stormy exhaust threatens to stampede the make believe toreador through the tunnel, and flatten him on the down-grade at Sydenham Hill.

Inside the long bore, the repulsive emission makes me take another look inside the white inferno. 'Well perhaps I should splash a bit more coal after all' . . . I think, blinded by the brilliant glow. The rapid evulsion consumes more coal than the fire could chew. I therefore fling four shovels full round the back corners to off-set the violent pull. Escaping the tunnel, Percy reduces power to a wisp, and I open the fire doors to let-go the lustrous glare.

At short length, Herne Hill, Brixton and Clapham are quickly surpassed, and there are no signs of the toreador. In the distance, the famous Battersea Power Station stands defiant, like an upside-down oil-rig, sticking its brick legs into the twilight belt. In the shadow of the power station, I screw both dampers down to congeal the fire. This practice, generally speaking, helps restrain the safety valves whilst standing in the station, providing of course, the fireman leaves room in the boiler to inject cold water to keep her quiet.

Whistling on past Stewarts Lane depot, the ongoing bend guides the train over the Thames to Pimlico, to where a steep (1 in 62) slope dips suddenly into Victoria. Henceforth, the driver applies the brake, not only against the descent, but also because of a cautionary signal. Finally, the complete train slows to a purposeful halt under a red light, a 'stone's throw' from the station platform. Our stop is

For me, an N class seemed more at home when it was in front of a heavy goods train than a passenger. Nearing its journey's end, No. 31405 is seen blowing off steam whilst traversing the Chislehurst Loop. The train is the 9.58 am Ashford to Hither Green freight.
13th February 1954   *Brian Morrison*

A passenger assignment from Victoria to Margate for N class No. 31413. Here, it is observed hauling a heavy train of red and cream Bulleid stock near Bickley Junction to pick up the Chatham route via Swanley. It would appear as though a 'Schools' or a Bulleid Light Pacific was not available on this occasion.
14th July 1951   *Brian Morrison*

There were 157 of the so-called 'Maunsell Moguls' built, and they came in four descriptions, the Ns, Us, N1s and the U1s; the former two having only two cylinders while the latter had three. Our picture shows a three-cylindered N1 class No. 31879 hauling (would you believe it) Pullman stock at Borough Market, towards London Bridge station. It is however Derby Day, and the train is off to Tattenham Corner, Epsom.

30th May 1951   *R.C. Riley*

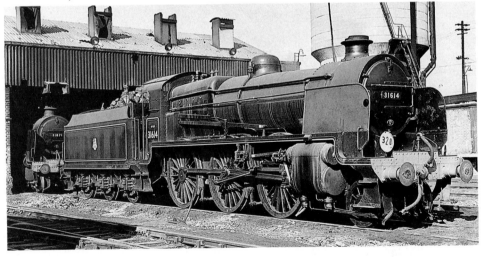

Like an ambassador sent to a foreign land, U class No. 31614 stands on road 8 at Bricklayers Arms, facing the turntable. No doubt it is waiting to be returned to the South Western section (after working a Meldon Quarry ballast train) and its home base at Bournemouth.

28th February 1957   *R.C. Riley*

Working up from Ashford to Bricklayers Arms via the Dartford Loop is N1 Class No. 31880. It is seen here belching out a rich exhibition of pungent filth adulterating the signal box, but luckily the signalman has his windows closed. The fireman leaning over the cab side is the author, staring at the photographer standing on Sidcup station platform.
24th June 1956   *Brian Morrison*

U1 class No. 31906 climbs away from Chislehurst on the 'down' local line to Dover. Here the three-cylindered engine is hauling ten bogies, but going by the hissing safety valves the fireman has everything under control.
8th November 1952   *Brian Morrison*

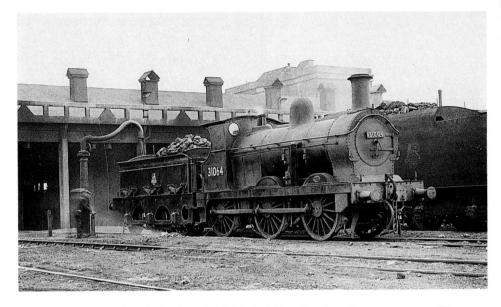

Seen here at Ashford is O1 class, 0-6-0 No. 31064 replenishing its water content. The antiquated outside tender springs and high handrail are worthy of notice, which made these Wainwright rebuilds of the O class easily identifiable.
22nd May 1954   *Brian Morrison*

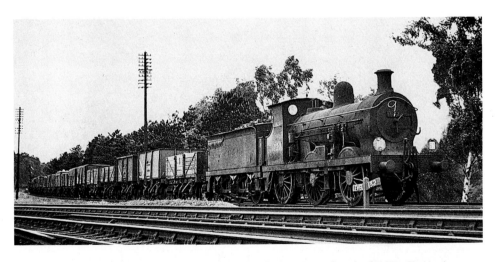

It was Harry Wainwright who produced the C class 0-6-0 for the SECR. From the 109 that were subsequently built from 1900, Bricklayers Arms was allocated 28 at their initial adoption. From this photograph of No. 31722, one can readily see that the class was really developed from the earlier designs of the O1 classes. On this class though the tender springs and low axlebox frames have been neatly tucked under the tender.
12th July 1951   *Brian Morrison*

Wainwright C class No. 31280 is seen standing in Bricklayers Arms shed. This was an engine I fired many times during the 1950s, pulling freight trains to and from places such as Plumstead and Angerstein Wharf. These engines were firm favourites amongst enginemen, and much preferred to the ex-LBSCR "Vulcan" C2Xs–unless you were a Brighton man of course.

11th September 1954   *Brian Morrison*

A C class just passing the Rotherhithe carriage sidings and the bright and gleaming North Kent West Junction signal box. According to the headcode No. 31293 is returning light engine from Angerstein Wharf, near Greenwich, making its way down the main branch line to Bricklayers Arms depot.

13th November 1954   *R.C. Riley*

A black day for the nearby residents at Tonbridge, but fortunately there is no clean washing out on the clothes line to the left. Here we see No. 31590, a typical example of a Wainwright C class, hauling a heavy coal train on the 'down' line through Tonbridge station.
26th March 1953   *Brian Morrison*

This somewhat squalid looking C class, No. 31725 is another B. Arms allocation. It is waiting for clearance to haul the goods train in the Well Hall sidings, near Bexley to Bricklayers Arms branch sidings. The fireman has positioned the correct headcode but he has forgotten to hook the front coupling on the bracket provided.
6th July 1951   *Brian Morrison*

A cut-down version of the R1 class 0-6-0Ts, No. 31339. The reasons for the lowered boiler mountings was to clear the roof of Tyler's Hill Tunnel, the first railway tunnel built in Kent, (near Canterbury). Even Robert Stephenson's *Invicta* was restricted because of its tall smoke-stack. The R1 is seen here at Folkestone Junction.
24th September 1955   *Brian Morrison*

Shunting passenger stock at Folkestone Junction sees a conventional R1, No. 31340, with its normal boiler mountings. Judging by its looks one can definitely observe it to be an ancestor of the H class tank engine. In the background is cut-down, No. 31339.
24th September 1955   *Brian Morrison*

For decades an H class tank became commonplace shunting passenger stock at Rotherhithe Road carriage sidings. A position almost as permanent as the signals shown in this picture. Of interest is the separate chain coupling slung over the front drawbar on No. 31533. This was a lot easier for a shunter to swing with his shunting pole.

31st July 1958   *R.C. Riley*

A number of ex-LCDR R class 0-4-4Ts survived into BR ownership and were used on various 'pull-and-push' services in Kent and Sussex. Here we have an example of one such service at Gravesend Central. As soon as the porters have finished loading the trolley, No. 31658 will then 'push' the two coach train all the way to Allhallows-on-Sea on the Thames Estuary.

20th June 1952   *Brian Morrison*

You can almost hear the continuous bark as this Standard Tank, No.80148, stretches round the bend at Peckham Rye with an empty stock train from New Cross Gate to Eardley sidings. The train is comprised of Bulleid coaches in green livery. The 4MT class 2-6-4Ts were more prominent on the East Grinstead and Uckfield routes to Brighton.

28th February 1957   *R.C. Riley*

The peaceful tranquility of the Surrey countryside is shattered when **BR Standard 2-6-4T No. 80086** 'blows off' a deafening roar, the tall white feather no doubt disturbing the natural habitat at Woldingham.

23rd June 1954   *R.C. Riley*

Ramsgate shed shows off No. 42106 a gleaming black LMS-type Class 4 2-6-4T. These were commonly known as the "Midland Tanks" because of their LMS connections and were clearly related to the BR Standard 4MT in both physical attributes and size.

November 1950   *Real Photographs*

A smaller, Ivatt designed LMS-type 2-6-2T, No. 41300 runs light through London Bridge station on its way to Bricklayers Arms depot. These 'cuddly' looking locomotives were often used to haul empty stock through London's south west suburbia to Victoria, and were nicknamed the "Teddy Bear Tanks".

13th March 1957   *R.C. Riley*

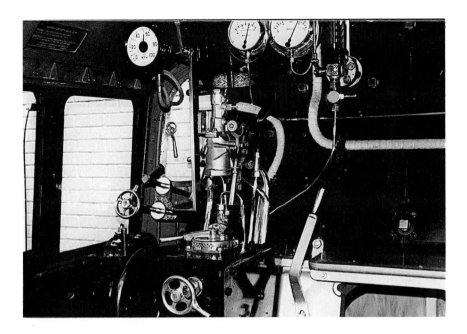

The footplate layout of the BR Standard classes as seen here at the National Railway Museum in York. Notice on the bottom left is a shining example of the "bacon-slicer" reversing gear, complete with rolling drum indicator. High above the gear control is the speedometer that was fitted to all BR Standards. On all other engines built before, the driver had to estimate his speed for there were no speedometers fitted.

23rd April 1987 *Author*

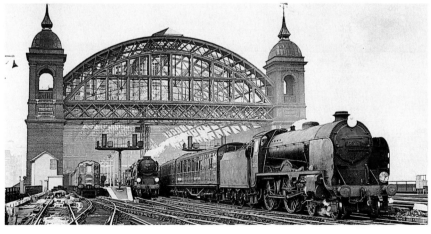

'Schools' Class No.30913 *Christ's Hospital* is seen here leaving Cannon Street for Hastings. The train is departing from platform 6 where just six months previously, a Ramsgate express left on its ill-fated journey in thick fog. The magnificent tall baroque towers have witnessed all trains coming and going since 1866.

30th May 1958 *R.C. Riley*

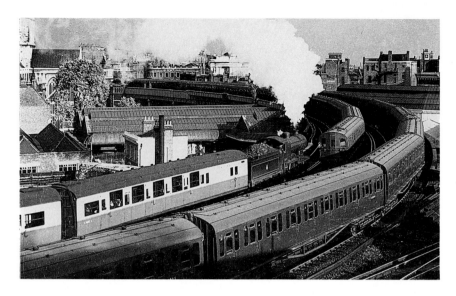

Rounding the hairpin bend at Cannon Street is D1 class 4-4-0 No. 31494 which is approaching London Bridge station. This route was the same that Driver Trew took on that foggy night in December 1957. The six driving wheels of 'Battle of Britain' class No. 34066 would have dragged the curve somewhat tenaciously. The on-coming green light (obscured by smoke in this picture) would have given him clearance through to London Bridge.

16th September 1955   *R.C. Riley*

The footplate controls that Driver Trew had to manage, (as seen here on No.34092 *City of Wells* at Haworth on the KWVR). The vertical regulator handle is clearly identified to the left of the two bottom gauge dials and because No. 34066 had undergone repairs at Eastleigh Works, the new regulator valve glands may have stiffened the handle.

23rd April 1987   *Author*

Just beyond New Cross station this picture shows the deepish cutting and bridges which Driver Trew had to face in only ten yards visibility. It was also on this impeded stretch that Trew passed two signals at caution. The 'down' main line is the second track from the right.
May 1986 *Author*

A driver's eye view just four seconds to impact. Here, at St John's station (main line platforms now removed) is the signal Trew passed at danger. His train went on to crash into the rear of the Hayes train stopped just yards the otherside of the flyover. The picture also shows the overhead line which Driver Corke was slowly negotiating two minutes after the impact.
May 1986 *Author*

The early morning light reveals the whole tragedy. A crane is about to lift part of the Hayes train free of *Spitfire*.
5th December 1957   *Photo Source*

This picture shows the collapsed flyover crushing the second coach of the Ramsgate train. The signals above the bridge are what Driver Corke was looking out for, and thankfully, he halted his packed commuter train just feet before the bridge subsidence.
5th December 1957   *Photo Source*

Just 18 months after the Lewisham rail disaster No. 34066 *Spitfire* is seen here at St Mary Cray Junction.
14th June 1959   *R.C. Riley*

An ostentatious British Rail logo oversights a 'down' Margate (emu), 4-VEP No. 7869 from Charing Cross, seen here stopping at Sevenoaks station. The elevated station buildings have all been finely remodelled – a far cry from steam days.
18th September 1986   *Author*

The emu seen here emerging from Priory tunnel, 4-CEP No. 1504, stops at Dover Priory before hugging the white cliffs through the Folkestone Warren. Worthy of special note must be the old signal box and outside 'loo' which still serves a modern purpose, if not a modern look.

September 1986   *Author*

This 'up' Margate train, refurbished 4-CEP No. 1587 in "Jaffa cake" livery, stops smoothly at Folkestone Central on its first leg to Charing Cross.

September 1986   *Author*

The attractive 'flash guards' throughout the train marry neatly into the locomotive. Here No. 73109 of Stewarts Lane is at the tail end of the fast return to Victoria of a push-pull 'Gatwick Express' working.

24th May 1987   *Author*

explained on platform 5, where a Bulleid Pacific is waiting to depart at the head of the 8.20pm to Dover. While we wait to change places with the 8.20, perhaps I may complement the next paragraph and explain the origin of such a 'steep bank' before the station.

Back in the 1850s, a proposition to build a new railway terminus was planned. The new line would meet up with existing track the south side of the River Thames which served the south eastern counties. Because of the steep land, it was suggested the station be elevated and a brick viaduct erected to meet level over the river. However, the upper-class residents of Pimlico had other ideas. They did not take too kindly to the 'very idea' of a brick monster in sight of their posh dwellings. Needless to say, their resistance won the day. So, Victoria was built and completed at 'ground' level in 1860. The inevitable climb to the river was called (and still is) Grosvenor Bank after the same named bridge over the Thames.

Just like London Bridge station, Victoria is really two stations in one. The west side serves the 'Old Brighton' and Central section to Surrey and Sussex, whereas, the East side serves the whole of Kent.

"A'ha!" movements on platform 5 see the Pacific engage the foot of Grosvenor Bank. The tremendous bark emits a roar far in excess of all the animals in the Battersea Dogs Home. Thundering upwards, the sound and smoke is eagerly pursued by another tumultuous pain, shoving the train from the rear and equally pumping out offensive garbage, not only over our train, but also into the face of tall adjacent housing. This custom is a usual procedure which gives the outgoing train a good start up the bank. It is amazing how much acceleration is attained by having an engine either end. As always, the banking engine stops short at the summit, and is then permitted to travel light for whatever duty required.

From the resident's point of view, I would sooner have a panoramic view of a brick viaduct, than a continuous bombardment of black and white thunderstorms sponging the windows at all times of the day, not to mention the noise and smell. Perhaps those bygone residents were blinded by their own selfish expectations.

A green light excites Percy's right hand. Blowing the vacuum brake off, the engine assists the train into the platform, gently encouraged by gravity. Inches off the buffer stops, Percy exclaims that we are 20 minutes late. Amidst a swarm of human bustle, the expected railway police are well positioned to nab the half a dozen soldiers who caused the train damage and because of this wilful damage, it is decided to take the train out of service. Therefore, we are requested to propel the ten empty coaches a quarter of a mile up the steep bank and into the Victoria carriage sidings, and thereafter, to run light engine to Stewarts Lane as per schedule.

It is a somewhat abnormal feeling propelling a long train in reverse, more especially on full regulator, up a steep bank. From the footplate the manoeuvre is completely blind as to where the train is going, we have to trust implicitly in the shunter riding the end carriage, who in turn ensures direction and brake control in case of emergency. The unexpected shunt, causes me to prepare the fire for the short sharp slog.

At last, the platform 'repeater' signal gives us the right-of-way. With a whistle and a prayer, *Launceston,* like the Duke of York, soldiers the carriages up the hill. Approaching the carriage sheds, at about 30mph, the impetus has then to be eased off, but not too much for fear of stopping foul across the main line. With that over, and darkness almost descended, we wait for road clearance to the depot.

Suddenly a militant combat pounds from the station. On passing the carriage sidings, the spearhead engine carries a circular frame which displays a crescent moon and the words "Night Ferry", across the smokebox door. This is the so-called "Blue Train" departing for Paris via the ferry at Dover Marine. The all blue coaches are of heavy French 'sleeper' stock throughout. The passengers go to bed somewhere in Kent, and wake-up to breakfast somewhere in France. The train was always double-headed because it was so heavy. Usually, a D1 class 4-4-0 led the way, being shoved by a Bulleid Pacific. Having watched the war-like battle disappear over Grosvenor Bridge, it is now our turn to go home to bed, somewhere in south east London.

Numbers and Names of the Bulleid Pacifics

'Merchant Navy' class

No.	Name
35001	Channel Packet
35002	Union Castle
35003	Royal Mail
35004	Cunard White Star
35005	Canadian Pacific
35006	Peninsular & Oriental S. N. Co.
35007	Aberdeen Commonwealth
35008	Orient Line
35009	Shaw Savill
35010	Blue Star
35011	General Steam Navigation
35012	United States Lines
35013	Blue Funnel Certum Pete Finem
35014	Nederland Line

162

35015	Rotterdam Lloyd	35023	Holland-Afrika Line
35016	Elders Fyffes	35024	East Asiatic Company
35017	Belgian Marine	35025	Brocklebank Line
35018	British India Line	35026	Lamport & Holt Line
35019	French Line C.G.T.	35027	Port Line
35020	Bibby Line	35028	Clan Line
35021	New Zealand Line	35029	Ellerman Lines
35022	Holland Amerika Line	35030	Elder-Dempster Lines

'West Country' and 'Battle of Britain' class

No.	Name		
34001	Exeter*	34037	Clovelly
34002	Salisbury	34038	Lynton
34003	Plymouth*	34039	Boscastle
34004	Yeovil*	34040	Crewkerne
34005	Barnstaple*	34041	Wilton
34006	Bude	34042	Dorchester
34007	Wadebridge	34043	Combe Martin
34008	Padstow	34044	Woolacombe
34009	Lyme Regis	34045	Ottery St. Mary
34010	Sidmouth	34046	Braunton
34011	Tavistock	34047	Callington
34012	Launceston*	34048	Crediton
34013	Okehampton*	34049	Anti-Aircraft Command
34014	Budleigh Salterton*	34050	Royal Observer Corps
34015	Exmouth	34051	Winston Churchill
34016	Bodmin	34052	Lord Dowding
34017	Ilfracombe	34053	Sir Keith Park
34018	Axminster	34054	Lord Beaverbrook
34019	Bideford	34055	Fighter Pilot
34020	Seaton	34056	Croydon
34021	Dartmoor	34057	Biggin Hill
34022	Exmoor	34058	Sir Frederick Pile
34023	Blackmore Vale	34059	Sir Archibald Sinclair
34024	Tamar Valley	34060	25 Squadron
34025	Whimple	34061	73 Squadron
34026	Yes Tor	34062	17 Squadron
34027	Taw Valley	34063	229 Squadron
34028	Eddystone	34064	Fighter Command
34029	Lundy	34065	Hurricane
34030	Watersmeet	34066	Spitfire
34031	Torrington	34067	Tangmere
34032	Camelford	34068	Kenley
34033	Chard	34069	Hawkinge
34034	Honiton	34070	Manston
34035	Shaftesbury	34071	601 Squadron
34036	Westward Ho	34072	257 Squadron
		34073	249 Squadron

34074	46 Squadron	34092	City of Wells
34075	264 Squadron	34093	Saunton
34076	41 Squadron	34094	Mortehoe
34077	603 Squadron	34095	Brentor
34078	222 Squadron	34096	Trevone
34079	141 Squadron	34097	Holsworthy
34080	74 Squadron	34098	Templecombe
34081	92 Squadron	34099	Lynmouth
34082	615 Squadron	34100	Appledore
34083	605 Squadron	34101	Hartland
34084	253 Squadron	34102	Lapford
34085	501 Squadron	34103	Calstock
34086	219 Squadron	34104	Bere Alston
34087	145 Squadron	34105	Swanage
34088	213 Squadron	34106	Lydford
34089	602 Squadron	34107	Blandford Forum
34090	Sir Eustace Missenden Southern Railway	34108	Wincanton
		34109	Sir Trafford Leigh Mallory
34091	Weymouth	34110	66 Squadron

* Bricklayers Arms (73B) allocations during the 1950s.

6
The Rise and Fall of the 'Schools' Empire on the '1066' Route

Being the ambitious and curious species that we are, the aspiration of the 'human computer between the ears' will endlessly pound indelible information that perpetuates the very foundations of discovered knowledge. I cannot imagine any terminal point in man's quest where everyone will say "Now we understand the whole thing". That of course will never happen. Thus, the sun will never set on man's unshrinking desires.

Examples in varied fields of modern science have indeed made satisfying inroads for the welfare of the human family. For example, many medical developments have facilitated support to prolong life and ease suffering. I suspect that there will be no end to that process, not only in the world of medicine, but in every possible aspect of human endeavour. Exploring and aiming to increase our understanding has been the pattern which has, without question, accelerated primarily over the last one hundred years.

Despairingly however, the dimensions of perception and founded knowledge are flagrantly overwhelmed by man's recurring ignorance which very often steers progression on a wrong course. Hence therefore, the wide and extenuating efforts of man, although fundamentally worthwhile, have thus been plagued with innocuous setbacks heavily outweighed by scintillating knowledge and negative foresight.

Over the years, many legal authorities have wilfully manipulated certain courses of action whereby, using their own governmental powers have forcefully dampened any visionary speculation, and their own excuse of scarce monitory resources justifies a reason. This was particularly true of our railway precursors George and Robert Stephenson, from the time both paid their own valuable contribution that purchased the scent of railway endeavour.

Over those early years of railway establishment, the rising sun of human frailty exposed many examples of mistakes which were forcibly acknowledged by disappointing results. But a man who never makes a mistake never accomplishes anything. Inevitably, many lessons were learnt back then, both good and bad which did, in effect, achieve improved but belated accomplishments. That sequel therefore must universally remain the paternal train that, without it, knowledge and understanding would probably be nil.

It seems apparent however, that many have found fault in the works of some bygone railway engineers. In recent years some critics have assumed an air of superiority which does lack conformal knowledge of the circumstances that were then under contention.

For instance, when the railway was finally completed from Tunbridge Wells to Hastings in Sussex in 1852, the civil engineers at that time could not possibly have foreseen the major barriers which they inadvertently caused for future railway traffic. Maybe it was for the same reasons the Romans did not envisage the coming of motorways. Obviously though, we have to conclude that the advent of a larger loading gauge was not then conceived and therefore, unforeseen. Consequently the bridges and tunnels on that route were constructed to suit those early compliances.

In the succeeding years when the loading gauge did become a set standard in Great. Britain, all coaching stock supplied for the Hastings route was custom-built to accommodate the existing confinements. A proposition to enlarge the tunnels etc., or to even remove them completely, was deemed far too costly and time-consuming and would therefore create as many problems as there were 'pebbles on Hastings beach'. Hence, the resilient and purpose-built stock.

Naturally, authorised written reminders were introduced and inscribed on all other conventional stock over 8ft 6in in width exclaiming its prohibition between Tonbridge and St Leonards. It was also recognised that the contemptuous restrictions impeded progression in terms of increased speed and longer trains. Although there was a copious selection of smaller locomotives available on the Sussex line, they were not suitably adequate in power to maintain the preliminary requirements to now cope with the surge of modern demand. Both the larger 'Lord Nelson' and 'King Arthur' class of engine no doubt acquired the power, but for reasons of their 'overweight' and 'square-peg' shape were inconceivable on the Hastings 'round-peg' route. Something had to be done, and very quickly, to keep abreast with the railways new quest and standard of conformities.

Richard Edward Lloyd Maunsell, successor to Robert Urie as

Chief Mechanical Engineer on the Southern Railway between 1923 and 1937, now became the fatherly figure required by the railway authority, to produce a modern class of locomotive for immediate express duties for the notorious Kent to Sussex line. At the same time, the new engine required capabilities of hauling up to 500 tons at an average speed of no less than 50mph to meet the ever-increasing passenger numbers and time-saving demands. A tall order indeed for Mr Maunsell and his task force of design experts. But yet another example of man's desire to upswing and develop his urge for improvement.

Moreover, reading closely between the then lines of railway financial wizardry, the hopeful prospect was perhaps encouraged with an added incentive of a panoramic restoration of monetory gain which had to be hailed as the real motive power behind the new programme. Surely that must be recognised as good business from the railway executives' point of view. Henceforth, the 'green light' was given for this visionary proposition to encounter speedily the impediment on the Sussex line. So it was that in March 1928 this imaginative and immaculate conception began.

Just two years later, in 1930, from the protective womb of the famous Eastleigh Works, was delivered a beautiful prestigious, iron baby, the V class 4-4-0, better known as the 'Schools' class. The prelude of apparent suffering and uncertainties carried by the 'mother' of railway officialdom was now over. Her newly-born stripling now independently alive and breathing its own smoke and steam was now raring to go.

The many new innovations deployed and utilised by the proud father showed the new machine to be in a class of its own – a 'chip off the Maunsell block' to coin a phrase. The weight at birth of 67 tons was most encouraging. The tender though, which weighed 43 tons was a converted six-wheel type that held 4,000 gallons of water and comfortably held five tons of coal. The illustrations of various 'Schools' show clearly how the side elevations were designed on both tender and cab which bent slightly inwards to facilitate the confines of the Hastings route. Both engine and tender in full working order gave a combined weight of some 110 gross tons, a much lighter locomotive as compared with other passenger engines that exceeded 140 tons gross. The three $16^{1}/_{2}$ x 26in cylinders gave a tractive effort at 85% of boiler pressure worked out at 25,130lb and thereby very capable of hauling the 500 tons originally required. The four only, 6ft

7in coupled driving wheels with their single-throw crank axle played a major role in fast and smooth running round the many curvatures, which minimised the effort against rail drag and a minimum curve radius of 4.32 chains was ideally suitable on the impeded route. I must say, a truly splendid masterpiece of Maunsell endeavour.

By 1935 however, a fleet of 40 of the new engines was thus built, a large family indeed for the Southern Railway. As the Southern handled a considerable amount of school traffic to both public and private boarding schools, it seemed appropriate to name the fleet after such institutions. So in view of the foregoing, the arched brass name plates which were fitted either side of the engine, and displayed above the splasher of the forward driving wheels, proclaimed the distinguished school's name, names such as, *Cranleigh, Dulwich, Harrow* and *Sevenoaks*, to name but four.

On 26th April 1930, numbers E900 and E901 made their debut at Charing Cross station on a Folkestone and Dover line service. The engines displayed *Eton* and *Winchester* names respectively.

Although primarily built for the Hastings line, it was to be another year of post-natal depression for the maternal railway forebearers before their new iron urchin could address the so-called 'Hastings Switchback'. For at this stage a few alterations and improvements were found necessary on the curvy permanent way between Tonbridge and St Leonards. The refurbishment of track alignment etc. was really in preparation for easy digestion to wean the new impeccable deliverer. By the end of June 1931, all was now ready to embrace Maunsells' 'Schools' class locomotive.

Henceforth, the new 'Schools', now reined securely to the longer and heavier trains, pursued the new valuable services with ease, no doubt a happy event for the open arms of railway officialdom. Accordingly thereafter, as from this date, the 'Schools' class was legally adopted as steam emperor in the south eastern Sussex domain.

Three sets of Walschaerts valve gear were employed in favour of the reciprocal gear of equal magnitude, and the performance proved exceptional. The remarkable energy produced and generated by this somewhat lighter and smaller locomotive proved significantly powerful, which was often undervalued, I am sure, by some B. Arms drivers I knew personally.

To detail what the 'Schools' were able to accomplish on the running road is tediously laborious, but the consensus of opinion among most enginemen has been that the engines manifested an outstanding display of proficiency in their work. When they were in good running order and in capable hands there could not be two opinions. It is worthy of note however, that the continuous use to which drivers put these most versatile machines demonstrated their genius and mastery of the highest order.

Over the ensuing years the 'Schools' blew smoke in the eyes of the then renowned 'Nelson' and 'Arthur' engines. Their own "Sirs" and "Knights" were forced to bow and were subsequently taught many lessons from the 'Schools' successful accomplishments. The quality and efficiency of the new engine to haul the 500 tons at up to 60mph on the aforesaid route certainly lived up to all expectations. Their acclaim therefore, was applauded by one and all, the rising sun of steam expansion had now reached its zenith, for the battle of Hastings was henceforth speedily conquered!

Inevitably in the years that followed a few teething problems became apparent, but not too seriously disconcerting. Some crewmen complained of drifting smoke which obscured visibility. Others at times were displeased with slow steaming performances. Naturally, modifications were thus carried out to help rectify the situations. In time however, 21 of the 'Schools' were fitted with Lemaitre multiple jet blastpipe and wider chimney. This no doubt enhanced the pull on the fire which in effect directly supplemented combustion to a higher degree and consequently escalated the steam pressure.

To combat the smoke problem, side vertical smoke shields were in turn fitted, one either side of the smokebox. This was for the purpose of deflecting exhaust smoke and steam above the engine and thereby allowing a wider margin of forward visibility.

During the 1950s, the motive power depot at Bricklayers Arms was allocated a wide variety of steam locomotives, a miscellaneous troupe of well over 100. Among those were as many as 18 of Maunsells' refined 'Schools' class which made up nearly half the fleet (a full list of names and numbers is situated at the end of this chapter). This beautiful creature was, in my view, a leading contender for the most elegant 4-4-0 ever to grace Southern metals. I in fact became infatuated with their well proportioned anatomy and refined behaviour, especially at speed when working the express services through Kent. The large driving wheels, graciously poised, seemingly glamourized their internal might, like a proud peacock strutting aloof. Their handling, as I rightly recall, was never a subject of discredibility, whatever the odds, their popularity never diminished and their spirited display echoed a true fondness with the men on the footplate.

Not surprisingly however, the 'Schools'' prestigious faculties reigned supreme at both Bricklayers Arms and St Leonards depots, an endurance of the highest calibre. The 'Schools', without exception, proved a personal favourite of mine, maybe because I worked this class more than any other, having the opportunity of firing to most of the fleet during the 1950s. In that same period British Railways decided to re-paint the majority of 'Schools' in green livery. Thirty-six were newly painted and the first to show off the new attire was No. 30907 *Dulwich* in July 1956. For reasons only known to British Railways, four of the class remained black; *Eton, Dover, Harrow* and *Blundell's*. I was not sure of my own colour preference, but no doubt both complexions enhanced the beauty of the beast, but then I suppose, beautification 'is only skin deep'.

Each engine's behaviour on the road very often determined at face value its own individual merit, but merit may only be obtained by crewmen exercising loving care and tender affection, coupled with a deep respect for all fast moving and working parts. A well known saying goes: "You only get out what you are prepared to put in". This principle is really true in all spheres of daily living, but it was particularly true of the relationship between crew and locomotive. Conscientious enginemen who were willing to exert extra effort in caring for their machine would not be disappointed. Often it was revealed that a well cared for engine returned the compliment, not by verbal flattery of course, but by a pleasing performance which spoke louder than words may ever express.

My own introduction to firing on the main line was first with a 'Schools' class locomotive. I must confess that on this first experience I found it extremely frightening. Trying to balance whilst placing coals, left handed, in a glowing firebox at 90mph, swaying and oscillating was an operation in itself. I soon discovered the footplate was not an environment for nervous agitators.

For a quarter of a century the reign of the 'Schools' remained unconquered and strongly entrenched in the Hastings domain. Their fortress was seemingly impregnable. It was not considered at all plausible that the Kent and Sussex protectorates, in the shape of the 'Schools', should ever be the subject of challenge. Sadly though, towards the end of 1955, the unbreachable became the most probable, for the 'Schools' empire was about to suffer a humiliating defeat. The sharpened axe of man's progression and founded knowledge stood aloft, threatening to cut down their white feathers for good. It would only be a matter of time to interpret the writing on the wall.

So it was that in 1955 the productive railway hierarchy carried the implement of death. Their hands stained with diesel oil, they officially translated the hieroglyphics that by the summer of 1957 steam would thus be ousted off the Hastings throne and be replaced by a new 'custom-built' stock of demu's (diesel-electric multiple units) which would now take over the 'Schools'' domain. To rub further salt into the now open wound, the then existing journey from London to Hastings would be chopped by 20 minutes by the new demus.

By the June of 1958 the new diesel-electric stock formed a new regime and enforced complete control. Yet another unfailing inroad for the welfare of railway endeavour. Defeat meant that black clouds would no longer have mastery over the Sussex countryside. For the sun had now set below the 'Schools' horizon casting an auspicious shadow over the ploy of modern technology, and the shadow of things to come.

In due course, however, the 'Schools' were in fact liberated and most of the family were commissioned over to the South Western section on parole where the sun shone favourably through their black clouds that deferred the axe of execution. They worked extremely hard on the Portsmouth and Bournemouth line services, often hauling 15 bogies well in excess of 500 tons. The last two of the fleet however, *Dover* and *St Lawrence* were permitted the final farewell before their own impending execution.

On 28th December 1962 No. 30911 worked the 4.40pm out of London Bridge station to Brighton in Sussex. After the journey's end she was then quite literally dumped, alongside three of her discarded sisters, (Nos 30901, 30915 and 30923) who were also waiting to be broken up.

In May 1963, No. 30934 *St Lawrence*, a 'Schools' I had fired on a number of occasions, returned to her place of birth to be finally axed, a pitiful and humilating defeat for a fine hard working lady. Thirty-seven 'Schools' were subsequently axed, with just three of the fleet remaining as a choice remnant for the purpose of preservation to this day.

It was in 1962 that the British Transport Commission officially affirmed that No. 30925 *Cheltenham* was their fancy for preservation. After a considerable time stored at Fratton, to the delight of steam enthusiasts everywhere, *Cheltenham* enjoys its new home at the National Railway Museum at York. Although over 200 miles away from its original Southern home, *Cheltenham* remains in resplendent glory, serving as an alien resident, a wonderful ambassador for Southern steam in the north of England.

Another 'Schools' I also spent countless hours with was No. 30926 *Repton*. This locomotive was purchased for preservation in 1967, the privileged buyer being the Steamtown Museum in the United States of America. After a complete refurbishment, its longer than usual journey west across the Atlantic, culminated in a home at Bellows Falls, Vermont. Her appearance was indeed altered somewhat, and dressed in a new western apparel it did perhaps resemble an undercover agent for an adroit diplomat noisely manifesting British steam. However, the locomotive was repatriated to the UK in 1989, ironically by an American.

It was Lord Montague of Beaulieu who paid the redemption price for No. 30928 *Stowe*. For fifteen long years *Stowe* remained as a cold interim reciprocator featuring a rigormortis display, standing rusting outside the National Motor Museum. Later it was shifted to the East Somerset Railway venue at Cranmore. However, official arrangements were thus made with Lord Montague for his kind permission to loan the 'Schools' to the Bluebell Railway at Sheffield Park, East Sussex, which, incidently, is only a whistle blow from the aforementioned 'Schools' empire. The good idea was to resurrect the engine back to full steam glory.

Extensive open surgery to respirate her internal organs was then performed by the engineering surgeons at Sheffield Park. The operation provided a medical bill of some £15,000, a sum three times the cost when originally built in the early 1930s. It was money well spent and most certainly not in vain, for in 1981 the all-important operation proved a complete success. *Stowe,* sporting her original number of 928, to the delight of all steam enthusiasts, returned to the land of the living, breathing once again her own delightful and sweet smelling smoke and steam. The new green livery blends nicely with the beautiful trees and fields of the East Sussex countryside. Although now somewhat confined at present, *Stowe* hauls a rake of Southern corridor coaches again, reminiscent of the 1950s, and takes short trips between Sheffield Park and Horsted Keynes, a journey of approximately five miles in each direction. A recommended ride for all lovers of steam. Another fine lady on the Bluebell Railway is an immaculate 'West Country' class locomotive which again, takes its turn on the same hop to Horsted Keynes and back.

It is a privilege to know though, that all three preserved 'Schools' were all at one time allocated to Bricklayers Arms mpd, where I spent many exhilarating hours in their exquisite company.

However, as recently as 1986, another example in the field of modern technology made yet another satisfying inroad – quite literally for the welfare of railway travellers on the Hastings route. From Tonbridge in Kent, the newly adopted and so-called '1066 Route' has employed yet another new ruler which purposefully now rejects all custom-built stock. The reason for this is because the offending tunnels have had both their double tracks ripped out and centralised by a new single-track to enable a comfortable passage for the new shape and colour of conventional width emus (electric multiple units).

South from Tonbridge station, trains to Hastings via Tunbridge Wells can now leave from either side of the station. A little beyond the station the line still branches acutely right from off the straight and fast main line to Ashford and Dover. Perhaps at this point we can ride an emu to Hastings and find out what new effects have taken place on the new '1066 Route'.

The Somerhill Tunnel, 410 yards in length was part of the 1986 electrification programme. The approach is a steepish uphill gradient and it is only single track, but used obviously for two-way traffic. Beyond this tunnel, the train continues swiftly along the side of a refreshing and beautiful green valley. Observing the undulating countryside one is immediately convinced that those early railway engineers had their work cut out in more ways that one. It certainly reveals evidence that Tunbridge Wells was a difficult place to reach with the steel rail. Steep gradients, a high, brick-built viaduct (Southborough), long cuttings and two tunnels. This stretch, nearly five miles long, remains much the same as it was in the steam days – minus the sight and smell of steam and smoke of course.

Soon after High Brooms station, the '1066' electric sprint sweeps effortlessly through the cuttings after Southborough, obscuring the view of the pleasing countryside, only to enter the 823 yards Wells Tunnel that emerges immediately into the platform of Tunbridge Wells station. (In steam days the station was known as Tunbridge

Wells Central). Straightaway, on leaving the station, the train slowly ducks under Grove Hill Tunnel, a mere 287 yards in length. Interestingly though, both Wells and Grove Hill tunnels are able to remain double track and the only alteration I can see is that the rail chairs in Grove Hill are now firmly embraced on a thick concrete foundation. This tunnel imposes a 10mph speed restriction however to repel any sway which might in effect encounter the 'still close' proximity of the tunnel walls. (Both tunnels had to remain double track for the purpose of the two-way platforms.)

A short distance beyond Grove Junction the line has also been single tracked, right through to the other end of another offensive bore namely, the 286 yards long Strawberry Hill Tunnel. Henceforth, and all the way to the outer skirts of Hastings, the track still acquires the numerous sharp curves and 'S' bends with which the old 'Schools' engines floated round with ease. Subsequently through Frant and Wadhurst stations, this section is now the highest point of the course. Next the train dips unrestrained into yet another single track section as it enters the depths of Wadhurst Tunnel, a black hole of some 1,205 yards length. Shortly thereafter, Stonegate, Etchingham and Robertsbridge are engulfed by more beautiful hills and green meadows. South of Robertsbridge provides the last of the once-impeded tunnels. Noticeably this tunnel of Mountfield, only 256 yards in length, came under extensive repair back in 1975, at which point it was then single tracked and given a concrete base in preparation for the already-planned electrification in the 1980s.

Our next point of call is the quaint Battle station with its stone and gothic style windows, exactly the same as it was in steam days. As a matter of added interest, Battle station was the architectural work of William Tress and was built in 1852. It is also remarkably sound, the construction being of very high quality, as indeed all the railway buildings are on that particular route which, incidently, reveal a variety of different styles of architecture and are well worth a purposeful visit. At Battle the choice is mediaeval, no doubt designed to blend harmoniously with the nearby Battle Abbey.

It is good also to see the old iron latticed footbridge, which spans the railway, still intact and in good use and painted appropriately in Battle green. When firing on the 'Schools', I always regarded Battle station as the place where the battle was now over as far as the shovel was concerned for the last few miles into Hastings gradually drop down to the sea.

Leaving Crowhurst station some sparse farmland and small river meet the eye with pleasing glimpses of the wide open sea afar, yonder some low and marshy land. A few twists and turns sway the train into West St Leonards which also marks the beginning of the Hastings built-up community and near to where the old loco sheds, now demolished, acquired the first twelve 'Schools' class engines which arrived there in 1931. On the bend through St Leonards lies Bopeep Junction where the well established electric line from Brighton and Eastbourne merges almost immediately into Bopeep Tunnel. This tunnel however, was aptly named after a local public house which was believed to have been used by thirsty shepherds who left their sheep for a pint of whatever. Whether they were able to find their woolly friends on their return is another story.

Bopeep Tunnel still remains double track of 1,318 yards in length and spills the train immediately into St Leonards Warrior Square station. This station resembles a classical mansion, unlike the station buildings previously referred to. The whole structure is of brick with stucco dressings, and enclosed with shallow pitched roofs.

Soon after Warrior Square, Hastings Tunnel, only 788 yards long, projects the emu neatly into Hastings station. Surprisingly, at this time of writing, Hastings still keeps the old semaphore signals and signal box, a glorious reminder of the days of steam. The station was first opened in 1851, and rebuilt in 1931. A fine but simple structure built in Wealden multi-red brick and contrasted with white stone dressings and cappings. The main entrance secures a flat roof, but the side and lower buildings have pitched roofs finished in red terra cotta roof tiles, typical of the 1930s.

It will be of great interest to note what modern science may further accomplish in future years. Perhaps 'nuclear' or even 'solar' energy may be the next 'emperor' to rule on the Hastings throne, who knows? For now though, it is circumstantially clear that electric motive power is here to stay for a long time yet and has silently stamped its authority as the supreme commander on the '1066 Route'. But sadly, with little charm and no chuff.

'Schools' (V) class 4-4-0

No.	Name	No.	Name
30900	Eton +	30920	Rugby +
30901	Winchester +	30921	Shrewsbury +
30902	Wellington	30922	Marlborough
30903	Charterhouse	30923	Bradfield
30904	Lancing	30924	Haileybury +
30905	Tonbridge	30925	Cheltenham
30906	Sherborne	30926	Repton
30907	Dulwich +	30927	Clifton
30908	Westminster	30928	Stowe
30909	St. Paul's +	30929	Malvern +
30910	Merchant Taylors	30930	Radley +
30911	Dover	30931	King's-Wimbledon +
30912	Downside	30932	Blundell's
30913	Christ's Hospital +	30933	King's-Canterbury +
30914	Eastbourne +	30934	St. Lawrence +
30915	Brighton +	30935	Sevenoaks
30916	Whitgift	30936	Cranleigh
30917	Ardingly +	30937	Epsom +
30918	Hurstpierpoint +	30938	St Olave's +
30919	Harrow +	30939	Leatherhead +

+ Lemaitre multiple jet blastpipe and wide chimney fitted.
Nos 30923-30939 allocated to Bricklayers Arms (73B) in the 1950s.
Nos 30925, 30926 and 30928 are preserved.

7
From Wainwright to Riddles

All depots had their own individuality and the ones I knew in the London area were no exception. It was my belief that we enginemen shared the same pessimistic view in having a tendency to look on the worst side of things, or at least to expect bad results. A doctrinal indifference which often oppressed enginemen's thinking, that their depot was the world's worst.

At the Bricklayers Arms however, there were regular compilations of customary duties using most of the older classes of engine which may have led to this impression. So from that point of view I will need more than the pages of this book to absorb each performance in detail, by which many momentous events will escape notice here. So I shall endeavour to piece together a brief historical evaluation of just a few engine makes; their individual origins, coupled with various duties which I recall in and around the fringes of South East London, which positively weakened the aforesaid psychological mood.

D1, E1 and L1 4-4-0s
One very memorable locomotive, originally constructed by Borsig of Berlin, was the ordinary looking L class 4-4-0. I say ordinary, for in my view it lacked femininity, a straight bulk with no real glamour, a solid mass of metal with only one connecting rod each side and fixed to two 6ft 8 inch driving wheels. The two cylinders, with their working motions, were confined under the boiler between the framework. But then, to be fair, I can only compare them with later and more elegant designs.

Only ten Ls were built in Germany, but later, another twelve were built by Beyer Peacock & Co. This static looking specimen came on the Southern scene in 1914, ironically just weeks before the outbreak of the First World War.

Their ability served the purpose well and they were considered powerful and fine through the war and for a while thereafter. Drawing attention to the weaknesses affecting future propositions of constituted railway planning, efforts to increase power became of paramount importance. Some older classes such as existing E and D class 4-4-0s, which were, incidentally, engineered by Wainwright and

Surtees just before 1900, were now on the cards for immediate alteration. Not only in larger size, but also an introduction of a 'superheated' boiler to keep abreast with the new generation of railway rejuvenation which began primarily from the 1920s and onward.

Due to Wainwright's resignation, it was our old friend Mr R.E.L. Maunsell who was then given the job of conversion and rebuilding. Although most of Wainwright's engines were re-built, the new regime inherited the nickname, "Converts", while the L class, because of their origin were dubbed "Germans".

Quite a few of the existing older breed remained in operational service, so it was decided that the new so-called "converts" had to be classified with the number "1" after the original class letter, becoming E1 and D1 classes. The E1 was first introduced in 1919, followed by the D1 in 1921. The larger L1 class was not initiated until five years after, in 1926 but, unlike the E1s and D1s these were built as entirely new locomotives, and were thus an addition to the earlier Ls. Apart from being a bit taller and somewhat pointed, the new remodels preserved a similar appearance and very little outward change from the original Wainwright design. Although I must admit Wainwright's Es and Ds were more elegantly defined with their characteristic 'hump-bridge' wheel splashers, which gave them a curvy look and perhaps were the best looking locomotives thus far.

Though a higher degree of development was incorporated by Maunsell, the new engines remained simple to operate, and certainly reliable. More importantly, though, they came out on top as far as increased power was concerned, quite out of comparison and able to haul anything up to 400 tons and very often more, if required to do so.

Almost to the end of steam traction on the Southern the Maunsell locomotives were kept in fine fettle. During the 1950s in particular, because of the application of even newer techniques in the shape of the more powerful 'Arthurs' and 'Schools' and not forgetting the might of the Bulleid Pacifics, the smaller "converts" were pushed aside and only used miscellaneously on trips such as I will now describe.

A weight restriction on Holborn Viaduct, across the River Thames (near Blackfriars Bridge), meant that nothing heavier than these 4-4-0s was permitted on or over the bridge. Thereby, a Maunsell rebuild was the only suitable engine to work the early morning 7am passenger train to Ramsgate. Usually, as I remember, the train consisted of only four carriages and maybe two or three parcel vans for distribution at scheduled stops on the way down. Quite an easy and manageable load for any "convert". A well sustained fire piled high under the fire-hole door kept the 180psi steam pressure well and truly satisfied.

The unique (James Stirling) steam-operated, reversing lever stayed the same, a small and effective instrument which was highly praised by all drivers I knew. It made possible a much higher level of everyday performance. The straightforward two lever movement, positioned comfortably at waist height, was a function as smooth and delicate as Brahms' Piano Concerto, but an added burst of steam, when changing gear of course, belched like a sudden wave in a sea of tranquility, and that was normal.

It was my experience to fire an E1 from London Bridge low level (Central side) with parcel vans to Dover over the 'Old Road', via East Croydon and Redhill. The only heavy part of the trip was the slog up Forest Hill bank, which I referred to in chapter three. The E1 galloped the near four miles bank with ease, like a wild stallion running as free as the breeze. But then, to be fair, we did have a good start over the arches before pummelling headlong through New Cross Gate to hit the bank at something like 60mph, leaving an intolerable display of black filth to fall over the Gate sidings, of which a greater proportion swept over our train.

Another prominent experience I cannot possibly forget was when working an E1 at the head of a very strange passenger train to Blackheath. The noisy, non-complaining passengers were really wild animals, both great and small, coming for their annual visit to Billy Smart's Circus. The 'Big Top' was always erected on the wide open heath, right opposite the Greenwich Park main entrance, near to where the London marathon now starts every year. By common consent it was a splendid sight to watch the mighty bull elephants striding with their slow motion gait the one mile to the big tent trumpeting under their own steam so to speak. For this reason, one local gentleman grew the best roses in the village!

Maunsell Moguls
These powerful locomotives, built inside a 17 year period, from 1917 to 1934, proved themselves very effective indeed, on both freight and passenger work. In fact there were as many as 157 built. The class

came in four descriptions, the Ns and Us and the N1s and U1s. The two former classes were built with two cylinders, and the latter pair with three cylinders.

During the 1950s, I had the privilege of working many a freight train with a two cylindered N class to places such as Tonbridge, Ashford, Faversham and Hoo Junction, as well as countless local duties. It was a satisfying feeling, particularly when pulling a heavy train out of the branch sidings, up the imminent bank to North Kent West and then, not surprisingly, to hear the safety valves suddenly advocate full release. Such were their steaming qualities. They also had a significant share of passenger work too, especially on summer excursions. Consequently, they were a good bet as a secondary standby if for instance, an 'Arthur' or a 'Schools' was not available for any reason. These exceptional and seemingly inexhaustible machines were an extraordinary feature, quite capable of hauling in excess of 500 tons. Once again Mr Maunsell was the chief 'master mind' behind their vociferous development, hence, the type became dubbed the 'Maunsell Moguls'.

On one particular Saturday Driver Sid Earl and myself worked an N from Bricklayers Arms as light engine to Blackheath carriage sidings. Arriving at the sidings we slowly backed onto our train for the local shunter to couple up. After road clearance we pulled the empty green stock the few yards into Blackheath station – but it was not to remain empty for long. A vast mixed company of mainly youngsters stood impatiently munching on ice cream and sherbert sticks. Their enthusiastic shapes and sizes could be described as a moving mass of uncontrolled energy. Some shone like the faces of angels, yet without question their actions divulged meaningful traits of the devil. In seconds the platform was deserted, for the train itself had swallowed the swarm of sticky-fingered urchins now poking their heads out of the open windows. Gladly, Sid and I were thankful to be safe on the footplate, away from the squall of these little young demons.

Starting away at about 10am, I recall that the weather was hot and humid, a perfect day for the seaside. Taking my jacket off I got ready for the somewhat daunting operation. We were scheduled to stop at most stations to Gillingham, via Woolwich and Dartford, and then all stations from Faversham to Ramsgate via Herne Bay. Although stops were very short, no more than a few seconds, the stop and start journey was to take more than three hours, so the poor kids would not have too long on the beach before having to return on the early evening train. But then that was the price one paid for the privilege of a 'cheap day' summer excursion. Frustrating though it was for the driver, the only advantage, from the fireman's point of view, was plenty of spare time between stops and spurts to negotiate water and steam supply. Taking this into account I made a generous provision of fuel each time we started away, inviting a tortuous black departure.

Shortly after leaving and entering Blackheath Tunnel, the injector decided not to work, blowing a trail of high pressure steam under the tender wheels. In my haste to re-operate, I looked down over the cab side, inviting a sudden gust to whip my shiny cap off and place it, green badge and all, somewhere inside the dank depths of the tunnel, never to be seen again.

Wainwrights C class 0-6-0s

Another turn, I clearly recall was when working the Plumstead goods train to Bricklayers Arms. It was mid-winter and very cold, and it was usual practice in the 1950s that a Wainwright C class was commissioned for the duty.

As can be seen in the accompanying photographs the C class was a development from the earlier designs of the Stirling O class and the inherent characteristics of the Wainwright O1 rebuild.

Just prior to the turn of this century, Harry Wainwright produced the C class for the then requisition to increase power. Though unmistakably similar, the main external difference from that of the O1, was the tender. The exalted outside springs and framework were a sight for sore eyes, but the new C class had these antiquated features well and truly concealed and, because of that, the long handrail high above the springs was no longer necessary.

Out of the 109, built from 1900 to 1908, Bricklayers Arms was allocated as many as 28 at their initial adoption. The footplate provided a neat and spacious area which afforded a long wooden box down one side to enable the crew to place their belongings inside. It also served as a comfortable seat for the fireman between firing. The firegrate was flat and so it was not the policy to bank the fire high up under the firehole door. An even spread, well alight, preserved the 160lb steam pressure very nicely.

Plumstead enjoyed a fairly large area of sidings which stretched alongside the main line, almost as far as Abbey Wood, thereby taking considerable time to shunt – a daily routine which became quite monotonous. The pilot engine spent most of the day shunting before working the late evening goods to B.Arms, a sparkling climax to an easy but often boring day.

The driver on this occasion was Bill Marsh. He was a quiet and likable sort with many years experience under his braces. As a serious yet enthusiastic railwayman he certainly knew how to handle a loose coupled train. During wintertime, his wife packed him off to work with a whole onion to eat with his 'cheddar' sandwiches. In the summer months the onion was swapped for a Cox's Pippin. In my mind's eye I can see him now, sitting comfortably opposite me on the footplate, penknife in one hand, thoughtfully attentive, slicing his apple (or onion) whilst we had our break during shunting.

Whichever sidings one worked, the added burden of winter cold and darkness created a hindrance which obligated the best vigilance from all enginemen. Along with a brave shunter, wrapped up in his winter garb, more so in pouring rain, this task demonstrated a skill beyond compare. Hence I will now take the opportunity to explain a sentiment of what shunting entailed under any weather conditions, good or bad.

Every shunter carried an oil lamp for the obvious purpose of signalling to the driver when dark. (Signalling codes of practice are found in chapter three.) Inside the shunter's lamp are one red and one green shade fitted securely to a swivelled metal cylinder. A flick of the wrist twisted the top handle which in turn altered the light aperture to the desired colour. It often amazed me the speed with which the shunter controlled his lamp, especially as he was dressed in heavy oilskins and hood, carrying a shunting pole in one hand and his lighted lamp in the other. Even then, he was still able to hook or unhook a wagon coupling, and simultaneously wave the required light with split-second precision.

One very outstanding operation, which demanded extreme skill, was when a shunter requested the driver to 'hit them up'. For example the idea was, that immediately after unhooking a number of trucks, perhaps on the move, the shunter would swing a white light rather rapidly from side to side, rather like a clock pendulum moving very fast. Bawling above the noise of steam and chuff, he shouted "Hit-em-up!" The driver, upon hearing the loud instruction, straightaway responded by opening wide the regulator to gain a fast momentum. Then suddenly, and expectedly, from the driver's point of view, the shunter flicked his wrist, and as quick as a blink, he offered a red light as still as a becalmed yacht waiting for a wind to blow. Needless to say when the engine jarred to a halt, the loose wagons catapulted independently into the desired road, where another shunter ran beside the trucks to pin the brakes down as soon as they cleared the opposing line. The only worthwhile purpose for this procedure was that it saved a great deal of time, and although not offically approved, it became a common and conventional method of shunting.

On one occasion I recall, whilst shunting at Angerstein Wharf, near Greenwich, amidst practical problems besetting shunters and the like, the driver propelled a loose set of wagons as described, but unfortunatly the 'greyhound' shunter slipped and fell face-down in deepish rainwater and mud. The uncontrolled wagons sped off to finally hit the buffer stops with an almighty crash. As well as bending the stops quite dramatically, three or four wagons leapt off the rails but remained upright at precarious angles. For the shunter, alas! Apart from a few uncontrolled words in opposition, he limped back to the shunters' lobby none the worse for wear, to dry out and bathe his wounds. But that was just one rare incident.

Fog and falling snow were the worst offenders, for the ears had to take the place of the eyes. Under those conditions of course, both driver and fireman were on constant alert, for there was no room for error, another sound reason perhaps for having a first-class knowledge of any siding. Most drivers let their fireman 'have-a-go' (driving) when shunting. In so doing I personally gained a wealth of experience, not only in handling a steam locomotive, but I also became familar with all the goods sidings in South London and suburban Kent areas.

From Plumstead via Woolwich the railway cuts through a black and austere environment of high brick-lined walls and short tunnels, a distance of some two miles or so. It was, and perhaps still is, an unappealing section, but having said that, maybe with an elegiac attitude, the pronounced architectural dimensions concealed in the cavernous structures retain their own beauty and charm which blend to form their own significant levels of ingenuity.

Our train consists of a mixed bag of freight of some 40 to 50 loose coupled wagons, and as usual the 'up' trip begins soon after the busy rush hour commuter services to the City.

Ready and coupled to our train, the departure dummy clonks off.

Bill pips the whistle and I spot the green light in the darkness from the rear end which explains the guard is ready and willing too. Driver Marsh therefore, cracks open the regulator to take up the slack progressively out of the train. With several slips and coughs of smoke, we make our way slowly across the down main line and snake into Plumstead station. Getting hold of the train, Bill immediately shoves the regulator to the stop plate and carefully alters the steam reverser which adjusts the arrangement of the violent chuff. Sighting the distant signal at 'all clear' I pull open the sliding fire doors. Grabbing the shovel I set-to and place three shovelfuls down one side and then the other, a couple under the door and back corners. Slamming the door shut I nick open the tilt flap which reflects the dancing fire and also illuminates just 130lb on the pressure gauge. A quick rake through and a bit more coal, soon has her steady on 150lb.

I always felt a tinge of excitement when seeing a regular rain of rockets and sparks. In the blackness of hollow caverns they reveal themselves strongly, eratically bouncing down off the short bridges and spraying wide, like an impressive Roman Candle on Guy Fawkes night. The fire-hole doors also beat their own refrain in perfect harmony to the exhaust tempo, for every chuff, chuff, rattle rattle, say the doors.

The white glare from the fire exposes a splended sight lighting up the sooted walls inside the short sharp burrows between the Arsenal and Woolwich Dockyard. The probing smell causes Bill to ask, in his jaunty humour, "Av-yer taken yer boots orff?" The cheeky monkey I think – not as bad as his onion breath!

Invariably the road is clear for a good run as far as Lewisham. Nearing Charlton station, Bill opens her out for maximum power for the impending up gradient towards and inside Blackheath Tunnel, now just three or four minutes away. At this stage however, the train has to be going like the wind (at least 30mph) if it is to gain sufficient momentum for the sustained half mile slog through the tunnel. Both steam and water are healthy when the C class ploughs unperturbed into the lowish confines of the black hell. Once again the Roman Candle declares itself immaculately spraying off the tunnel roof, but Bill and I make sure our heads are kept well inside the cab.

On the approach to Lewisham the road is relatively easy-going, but then cautionary measures have to be perfectly correct, more especially hauling a loose coupled train about to enter the busy 'spaghetti loops' at Lewisham and Parks Bridge Junction. Bill shuts off steam at Blackheath, mainly in response to two yellow lights staring at us just beyond the station. As usual, it seems we are going to stop in Lewisham station, no doubt to give priority to commuter traffic to and from the City.

An initial rub on the vacuum brake leans the train on the tender and pushes us on with an obvious lurch past the next 'one yellow' aspect. Our William cleverly releases the brake momentarily to stop the wheels 'picking up' which could transpose our conveyance into that of a toboggan on a slippery slope. High above Lewisham Road, Bill asks me to screw the handbrake on a touch as an extra precaution. In so doing I cannot help noticing the lights over the Gaumont cinema advertising a panaromic display of Clark Gable in "Gone With the Wind". Stopping in front of the red light on the platform we wait, but the safety valves lose their patience and, despite my efforts of control, they remind all around that we have a full head of steam. At last a 'one yellow' quickly changes to green. Descending the short ongoing bank one can literally feel the guard doing a superfine job in holding his brakes against our pull through St Johns.

The short and snappy trip finishes its course at Bricklayers Arms sorting sidings. We then run light engine to the loco shed where another crew take charge to dispose and prepare the C class for the early morning coal working to Hayes in Kent.

Many coal merchants, more so in the 1950s, operated their businesses from the comforts of a railway siding, and so it was that daily supplies were thus delivered. One popular route was the Mid-Kent line to Hayes where the line terminated. This section was one of a few branch lines, which from the 1930s was primarily dominated by electric multiple units (emus) to and from Charing Cross and Cannon Street.

However, in the wee small hours a crew began their day's work taking a C class from B. Arms depot to the branch sidings and pick-up a string of coal trucks laden high with 'household nuts'. In wintertime it was a sound bet that the guard pinched a bucketful to keep his brake stove going for warmth during the trip. Underway, Catford Bridge was naturally the first stop en route. After shunting in the somewhat narrow siding alongside Doggett Road, it was the usual custom to go and make the tea in the small 'dolls house' signal box on the opposing side. What was accomplished at Catford was, in due course, repeated at nearly all sidings to Hayes. Hence, the work was completed a few hours later by which time we ran back to Elmers

End for our break.

After a hearty breakfast of Kraft cheese slices and a fresh can of tea, we completed the night's work in the daylight, shunting Elmers End sidings. With that over we waited our turn between electric trains, for the mad dash (tender first) returning light engine to B.Arms, where we ourselves disposed the engine before cycling home to bed.

The C class was certainly a fine and powerful lady that was much more favoured than the open and draughty C2X (Brighton) "Vulcans". Interestingly, for all enthusiasts and the like, a prime example of a Wainwright C class BR No. 31592 is immaculately preserved at Sheffield Park, and is often seen working in full steam glory, polished dome and all, pulling passengers on the Bluebell Railway.

H class 0-4-4 Tanks

In the early 1900s, problems connected with increased traffic around London led to the introduction of yet another new locomotive class. In contrast to the splendour of the D, E and O classes of engine, Wainwright developed a small but powerful tank engine, an 0-4-4T. It proved a great success having far-reaching abilities, which to a large degree overcame the above problem. Going by its looks, however one can definitely see that it was a direct descendent of the R and R1 classes. All the Hs were subsequently constructed at Ashford Works in Kent. Thus, out of the 66 built, from 1904, Bricklayers Arms received twelve when initially allocated.

For decades an H class became commonplace, shunting the Rotherhithe Road carriage sidings at the top end of B.Arms branch sidings near Corbetts Lane. A position almost as permanent as the brick viaduct which ran alongside. On two or three occasions, during the mid-fifties however, I was booked as fireman with the then regular driver, (a name I forget). One particular aspect I vividly recall was an extended steel arm purposefully bolted to the regulator handle. This useful implement was a unique and purpose-made handle, made I believe, by the late Henry ("Harry") Turner, an engine fitter at B.Arms repair shop. Though not related, Harry, and his mate Bob Bell were great friends of the family and both were game for a 'chinwag' if I happened to be passing the shop on my way home, providing they were not too busy of course. The purpose of the extension was to save the driver stepping inside the footplate centre to close or open the regulator every time an order came from the shunter to either stop or go. Without the extension, the driver could easily lose sight of the shunter, or wear himself out in the bargain, 'to-ing' and 'fro-ing' at every move. Thereby, the extension provided a handy means to manage the regulator from the cab side and, most importantly, to preserve external vision at all times. A pity Wainwright didn't think of it in the first place.

Also, because of the automatic steam reverser, similar to that fitted on the C class, a driver would often choose to hold the regulator open and reverse the engine without stopping. A sudden cough and a jarred jump, and the H class was off again into which-ever direction the driver engaged. A practice not officially recommended.

Although only a small tank engine, the H class was very capable of hauling as many as twelve heavy carriages. Their stamina and strength was tested regularly up the steep bank beside Rotherhithe Road arches, where, a few hundred yards on it met level with the main Greenwich and Chatham line. With determination and skill, both the engine and driver, adhered super-abundant qualities dragging the heavy stock, though slow, against the pull of gravity. The purpose of the shunt however, was to permit a main line locomotive to couple-up on the other end. Stopping under the red light on the bank summit, perhaps a 'Schools' or a 'Light Pacific', then coupled to the rear. After exchanging whistle blows and obtaining a clear road, both engines pushed and pulled the empty stock out onto the 'two-way' line before North Kent East signal box. From here, atop the arches, the main line engine controlled the stop behind the signal gantry. Climbing down off the footplate, and cautiously stepping over the live conductor rail, I unhooked both vacuum pipe and coupling, in that order. Another whistle exchange informed the other driver (now in forward position) that all was ready for him to make a brake. On receiving a green light, the main line locomotive pulled away the empty train in the opposite direction, across the points to intercept the local 'up' line towards London Bridge. If you have not already guessed, the carriages were off to either Charing Cross or Cannon Street to form a 'down' passenger train to the Kent Coast. But for the driver, myself and the H class, we followed closely behind the ongoing train only to stop clear under the same signal gantry and wait clearance to return down the short bank to continue our shunting, or perhaps repeat the same operation.

The H class were widely used, not only from Bricklayers Arms, but all over the South Eastern section. They were apparent favourites on numerous pull and push trains, having to work short hops and sprints with two to four carriages on many branch sections in and around Kent and Sussex. Such branches as Gravesend to Allhallows, Paddock Wood to Maidstone West, Tunbridge Wells to Oxted, and many more, too many to mention here. Throughout their life, and according to my own experience, I can only say they were exceptional. Like the C class one survives and can now be seen on the Bluebell Railway.

Riddles 'Standards'

From 1948, due to Nationalisation, British Railways was thus formed. Maunsell had gone, and Bulleid, who retired in 1949, was the last Chief Mechanical Engineer, and henceforth no more 'Southern' engines were acclaimed.

Though the advent of electric and diesel traction was very much in the wind, steam it seemed, still had quite a few puffs of years left. The evidence was very clear, everywhere one went, steam engines manifested themselves well, pushing easily against the coming 'armageddon' storm.

R.A. Riddles was certainly a man of high repute. In practical terms he was an accomplished engineer both in engine workings and design. He was brought up as an apprentice at Crewe to C.J. Bowen-Cooke on the London & North Western Railway as early as 1909 to 1914. His remarkable personality and deep interest in the railway philosophical system injected in him a thick railway blood, a physical phenomenon which remained with him through and through.

Furthermore, his practical and personal aptitude was first evident during the 1911 Railway Strike when he put himself forward as a substitute fireman, and later in 1926, this time during the General Strike, he promoted himself as temporary driver. He really began his career as a fitter on the LNWR after serving with the Royal Engineers in France soon after the World War I. In addition, much experience was also acquired in the United States of America just prior to World War II. No doubt the knowledge gained stood him in good stead for his continued work in Great Britain. Not exactly a babe as far as railway ethics were concerned.

Perhaps his most notable achievement was hallmarked during World War II which brought him his greatest acclaim. During that period, conforming to war restrictions of course, he developed, in conjunction with the North British Locomotive Company, the so-called 'Austerity' classes of which hundreds were built. For that ambidextrous 'cut price' accomplishment, Riddles was awarded the C.B.E.

During the new tide of nationalisation, Riddles became Vice-President of the LMS, a distinctive and responsible role, having authority over the complete motive power complex. Being on the British Railway Board of Executives, he was therefore well placed in the outcome of future developments. Despite the ultimate eventuality of electric and diesel traction at length, Riddles imagined a wide expanse between steam and the complete enforcement of the new up-and-coming regime.

Not only was he an economic theorist, but was seemingly, from my point of view, a student also of human behaviour and political thought. Therefore in relation to that, a new series of BR Standard classes was built which reinforced and enlarged 'steam' traffic, although perhaps more noticeably I feel, on the ex-LBSCR lines. There were in fact as many as twelve types subsequently constructed, but during the 1950s at Bricklayers Arms, I only recall working on four types, and those were as follows:

Class 4 and 5 4-6-0 tender engines.

Class 4MT 2-6-4 Tank engines.

Class 2 2-6-2 Tank engines dubbed the "Teddy Bears'.

To illustrate their marked approval, perhaps we can join a Standard Class 4MT at East Croydon on its last leg to London. Our train is a prestigious early morning business train up from the fashionable resort of Brighton. The journey so far has been a swift and deliberate effort, principally, because Alf Vandyke was that kind of driver. For me, although having only seven carriages behind, the real hard work was now over. Just a final race to Forest Hill, and from then on, the train was quite capable of taking itself the next five miles to London Bridge with very little help from the regulator.

It was a cool and pleasant morning, the sun low over Croydon. In contrast the steam pressure was rising high, the needle flirting on 220, just 5lb below maximum. Shutting off the injector, the water bobbed comfortably one inch below the top nut and we were ready for the off. The guard waves his green flag the way a cricket umpire gestures for six, and his pea whistle gargles in firm support as a final pinstriped gentleman flings himself aboard. Alf pulls the regulator wide and hangs his hat on the end and grins a crafty smile across the footplate. The heavy exhaust does not fall away until Alf rolls the (bacon slicer) gear lever back, as we pass under St James Road, a few hundred yards on.

With an inspired ceremony and a certain formality, our rapid speed comes almost as quickly as any electric train from full stop; and rarely did a Standard slip. Our thunderous gallop rounding the left curvature hurtles the train under the Tennison Road bridge to take the straight run through Norwood Junction station at 60mph, which is registered on the new speedometer. There is no more need to further fire, for I have sufficient fire for the remaining leg. Plus I know Alf will be shutting off steam at Forest Hill to descend the 1 in 100 bank to New Cross Gate. Flashing past Sydenham I put the injector back on and Alfred progressively pushes in the regulator, withdrawing his hat at the same time, placing it in its proper place. The speed now registers over seventy as we career down the bank by which Alf closes in the regulator completely. The green lights allow us to further excel our speed to 80 on the clock. One can feel the smooth and well oiled roller bearings inviting a gentle sway of the engine diving quietly past Honor Oak Park, as graceful as a kingfisher plunging for its prey, except there was no water.

Brockley comes into view, and it seems criminal to watch Alf check the speed in preparation for the 65mph limit at the Gate. A scream on the whistle lifts us under the road bridge at New Cross, but driver Vandyke once again opens the throttle a whisper to maintain the speed, passing the high signal box to our left. Unconcerned, I close off the injector and adjust both dampers accordingly. Sweeping over the B. Arms branch and the carriage sidings, we hastily meet the merging Chatham line and the usual smell of chocolate and baked biscuits. Then, a signal check brings us right down to earth, but then Alf says "Cor blimey mate – we're three minutes early!" The oncoming 'one yellow' light informs the driver there is an obstruction on platform 14. Sure enough, our slow entry foresees a parcels van tucked up against the buffer stops.

Not waiting for us to stop, the majority of 'bowler hat and brief-case' gentlemen hurry past as Alf stops the engine about six feet off the van. Most passengers are not interested in our shiny black engine which has just brought them safely from Brighton – miserable lot I think, perhaps because it was a Monday morning. Alf has the last say, with a wry and prudent smile he releases the steam operated cylinder cocks. The momentary roar envelopes the poor parcels van which disappears completely from view and some passengers sway their bodies to escape the white blanket.

All Riddles' Standards were firm favourites and a joy to work on. Whilst one must acknowledge the 'sweet' and encompassed technological advancement, we cannot truly disregard the powerful wonders created by steam over a 150 year period. Perhaps that celebrated riddle quoted on every Tate & Lyle syrup tin should conclude my final sentiments: "Out of the Strong came Forth Sweetness".

8
Five Miles and Four Seconds to Disaster

In relating this tragic incident, I must stress that I have no desire whatsoever to rekindle the suffering caused, or to revive painful memories for close relatives of those who died. My main purpose is simply to illustrate one man's unfortunate error, and how easily such an accident can happen to almost anyone in similar circumstances. This minute by minute account will hopefully reveal to you, the reader, certain facts which, in my opinion, played a major role in what happened.

My scenario begins on a cold, dark and foggy evening on Wednesday 4th December 1957. The somewhat dismal venue was London's Cannon Street station which was built on and above the north bank of the River Thames. On platform 6 stood a 'Battle of Britain' (unrebuilt) Pacific (No. 34066 *Spitfire*) at the head of an eleven coach train, the 4.56pm to Ramsgate (via Dover) waiting departure. The bleak and foggy conditions were not pleasant, especially if you happened to be standing on platform 6.

Overlooking the shrouded scene were an immense pair of tall baroque square towers positioned either side of the station, thrusting their Babylonic dominance heavenwards. They resembled two brick obelisks, a constant feature perhaps, of a fine British engineer, Sir John Hawkshaw. The metal arched roof spanned its 190 feet enclosure claiming anchorage to both tower lords, offering very little protection to passengers and staff alike who waited patiently for their trains. The fog gave an air of gloom and despair for many persons who were delayed by the turbid intrusion.

Driver Trew and Fireman Hoare, both Ramsgate men, were assigned the ill-fated 4.56. They were just two of the unfortunates forced to freeze on platform 6. Furthermore, they had earlier worked a train from Ramsgate to London, and had by then completed five hours of duty. Their arrival at Cannon Street was well in front of the scheduled departure time, obviously hoping for a right time start. But that was not to be for the weather hindered events, extending their wait on the platform to a lengthy 75 minutes before their engine appeared at 5.55.

With wholesome respect, Driver Trew was not a young man, his 62 years was not ideally suited to standing in that cold environment. It is obvious that he must have felt painfully cold, not conducive for maximum alertness at the controls of an express train carrying hundreds of trustworthy passengers. However, Driver Trew had no alternative and the 4.56 was not the only train delayed because of the fog. All schedules were unavoidably disrupted, for similar problems existed at the nearby Charing Cross station.

Boarding the footplate, Driver Trew was informed by the Bricklayers Arms driver (Charlie Jeffries) why the present water content was only 50% capacity. What was Trew to decide? A tender only "half full" was nowhere near enough for the trip, even less so in those foggy conditions. One could never foresee how much time would be used up, any delay would drink up the vital water content. Even a full tender may not have been sufficient on this occasion! Nevertheless, a prompt decision had to be made. What made matters worse was that there were no water facilities on the adjacent platform. The arch-enemy "Time" drew his sword. After a quick cut and thrust with time, Driver Trew agreed to make an unscheduled stop at Sevenoaks, 21 miles south, to fill the tender with water. No doubt a favourable decision in normal conditions, but not such a good idea in the current hampered conditions, although each driver must be master on his own ship and decide for himself the best and safest course of action.

Half a mile away, through the foggy streets of London Town, within sight of the celebrated dome of St Paul's Cathedral, are the unmistakable signs of Fleet Street, the nucleus of world news. The printers no doubt busy conjecturing reports for their impending daily rag. For, unknown to them, at that hour, their intrepid headlines must herald a different story.

It is difficult to appreciate, in the world in which we live, that thoughtfulness and consideration are lubricants that oil the machinery of human relations, and are a sure foundation for erasing many human errors and accidents, as well as solving most, if not all, of the world's agonising problems.

Experts well versed in the field of safety control have unanimously agreed that over 90% of all accidents could be prevented if the aforementioned virtues were liberally and lovingly administered. However, man generally lacks a deep respect for the sacredness of life and a 'genuine' love of neighbour and therefore governmental authorities have thus been judiciously enforced to introduce a variety of accident preventative measures. In some industrialised nations this began during the first half of the 19th century.

Back in the 1840s, many authorities and businessmen began to recognise how harmful accidents were becoming to their communities. Economic setbacks through loss of working hours, medical expenses, damage to property and merchandise, not forgetting the adverse psychological effects, made accident preventative measures urgently imperative.

For the railways in particular, governments gave authority to the Board of Trade to select and commission Railway Inspecting Officers. Their main objectives were to legislate a controlled and careful vigilance which could convey and supersede on any new line, developments only operative by their mandatory concessions. They were also responsible to investigate scrupulously and probe into the causes of all railway accidents and assess impartially their findings. The reports over the years have revealed that these appointed officers have afforded lavish ideals that have positively reinforced safety on our railways, and continue to do so.

In the early days of railway operations, particularly in Great Britain, serious accidents were generally non-existent. Perhaps it was the low speed and little traffic which contributed to that early safety record, but as time went on, so did rail development. With increased demand, this inevitably narrowed the margin of safety. By and large, it would seem that human error is strongly influenced with ignorance, selfishness, impatience and carelessness – four fundamental characteristics which cause most accidents. In many countries, a fatal accident by a person who disregards safety regulations whether by road, rail, sea or air, can result in criminal, manslaughter charges. In one second a horrifying accident can happen. Although over in a flash, their effects can last a lifetime, disturbing traumatically the lives of many.

Over the years, many safety laws have undergone complete refurbishment to suit and adapt to the many technological developments in relation to man's never-ending progression. Although parliamentary endorsed, these present laws have produced habits consistent in safety control which have saved life and limb.

Recent statistics reveal that only a small percentage of all accidents can rightly be attributed to the unforeseen, as well as to uncontrolled human fallibility which has a wilful effect on bodily direction and control. It is with this mental sphere of observation that I wish to emanate my own revelation, without prejudice, of why Driver Trew permitted the Ramsgate express to pass a 'red light', subsequently killing 90 passengers.

Returning to Cannon Street, the signal at the end of platform 6 displayed a green light. The time was 6.08pm, not enough time for Driver Trew to start to feel warm. Contrary to assumption, the footplate is not always the warmest place to be. Sighting the guard's light to the rear, the driver acknowledged the guard's right of way, just 13 minutes from boarding and 72 minutes behind schedule.

The steel regulator handle may have been tough for cold Trew, for two months prior, No. 34066 underwent surgery at the Eastleigh Works, and perhaps because of their newness, the valve glands were too tight for comfort. Leaning forward for maximum pull, two hands may have been necessary to yank the regulator open. Slowly but surely, the steam pressure forced the pistons to yield. Simultaneously, the six driving wheels firmly motioned forward. The coughing smoke and exhaust fumes increased dramatically, calling the tune to the coaches following without complaint, to the illustrious beast.

Its vermicular course over crossovers and points allowed the smoke and steam to mingle with the ever-present shroud that obscured the now-disappearing twin towers and crescent roof, that had witnessed all trains coming and going since 1866. Happily, a familiar smell of hops and beer escaped the local brewery that secured a tinge of pleasantness to the brumous surroundings.

The regulator would now be fully open with little cut-off on the gear lever, allowing maximum power to haul the brute weight (500 gross tons) and the train's lean against the steep cambered left hand bend. Steel wheel and steel rail whistled tenaciously, screeching their opposition in mortal combat. The green light on the south bank opposite the signal box indicated right of way into London Bridge station. The speed, as the train arched its back into the merging Charing Cross line, may have crept to only 15 to 20mph.

A few minutes earlier a Charing Cross to Hastings train and an electric Hayes train were only a short distance ahead, commanding the same foggy route. A right hand curve and a shallow down gradient allowed Trew to increase the cut-off percentage and, because of the persistent fog, ease down the acceleration, as the momentum pushed the train quickly through London Bridge station. The gentle beat of the exhaust informed Trew, that the valve cut-off was about right.

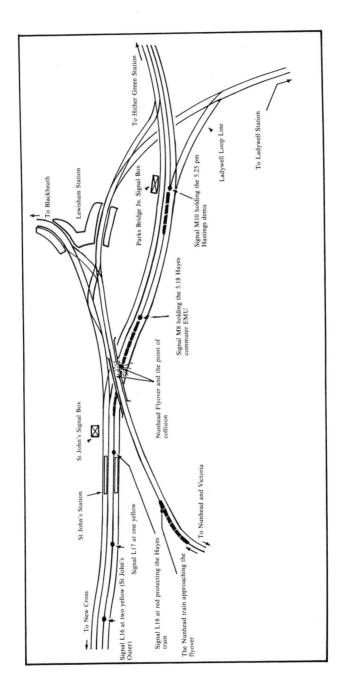

Track Layout and Signal
Positions of the
Lewisham Train Disaster   4th December 1957.

Within the figure:

To Hither Green Station

To Blackheath

Lewisham Station

Parks Bridge Jn. Signal Box

Signal M10 holding the 5.25 pm
Hastings demu

Ladywell Loop Line

To Ladywell Station

St John's Signal Box

Signal M8 holding the 5.18 Hayes
commuter EMU

Nunhead Flyover and the point of
collision

St John's Station

Signal L17 at one yellow

To Nunhead and Victoria

To New Cross

Signal L16 at two yellow (St John's
Outer)

Signal L18 at red protecting the Hayes
train

The Nunhead train approaching the
flyover

With no mistake the shrill cry from the engine whistle, plus the sound of the rolling train, hindered the amplified voice announcing all stations to Dartford for passengers boarding the commuter train on platform 2. The fire on *Spitfire* would now be satisfactorily invigorated. Fireman Hoare, an experienced main line fireman, at this stage perhaps, intending to add fuel to the white hot inferno and inject water into the boiler to facilitate demand for the next green light, may have encouraged him to initiate combustion control in accord with the driver's imposition. He may also have had in mind the long haul from St John's station up to the North Downs and Knockholt, an overall climb of twelve miles. Although the tempo at the moment was congressionally slow, postulation was not the name of the game, for one must never take any situation for granted. Although circumstances were far from normal, an occasional steam blow-off was thus unavoidable, and should be forgiven, rather than a condemnation for wastefulness.

The Ramsgate passengers, realising they were at long last on their way were no doubt looking forward to arriving at their respective destinations. A slow 'diddle-e-dum, diddle-e-dum' echoed satisfaction as each settled down for the less than two hour journey. Smoke and steam must have cajoled the carriage windows, whispering blank flirtations in silent adulation. Many passengers, perhaps with their eyes closed, exhaled abstract "zeds" as soundless as the external fog. A light snack and hot drink may have satisfied a need for some, and others may have chatted, played cards, or simply browsed the evening papers, a comfortable way to relax and pass the time.

The draughty footplate was a different scene. The crew must not relax, for the atmospheric conditions demanded more than the usual attention, and every signal in their turn had to be purposefully sought after. Under clear conditions though, signals from London Bridge were visible as far as the eye could see. An elevated motley of horizontal coloured lights navigate a plotted course, and deliberate effort is therefore spared.

Trew's speed must have been progressively slow, what with the impeding weather. Well over an hour late, Trew must have been quietly frustrated; being forced on the ropes, to coin a phrase.

Part of a driver's knowledge is to have the ability to recognise every installation on the permanent way. Not only by sight and shape, but more emphatically by the sound picked up through the wheels of the locomotive. For example, crossovers and points, under bridges and over bridges, short tunnels and long tunnels and many more. All will have their own distinctive hue of interpretation. This knowledge is imperative and essential when working over sections in foggy and other adverse situations.

Driver Trew of course was no exception, he had already clocked up 18 years experience as driver. It was reported of him that his maturity and ability was first rate, a "grand master" in the truest sense of the word. His colleagues at Ramsgate depot described him as a loyal and conscientious servant with a good sense of humour, but not perhaps as sprightly or quick thinking as others, but that was not at all considered a detriment to his ability. He was a typical engine driver, a career man, a man who loved the railway and resigned himself to a lifetime of railway servitude. He knew only too well, as we all knew, that the rules had to be strictly obeyed. That it was important for railway employees to appreciate that their own safety, as well as that of the passengers, was subject to all regulations, and most importantly to maintain a restrained sentiment. Time was not the essence; time must always play second fiddle to passenger safety. The lives of passengers were the repertoire that demanded three-fold qualities from every crewman: (1) Physical and mental endurance. (2) A high standard in literary ability. (3) An unconditional and unselfish attitude. Why therefore, did Trew permit his train to follow a path of destruction?

To answer this question, we have to consider another side to human behaviour that is not fully expounded in textbooks. Understandably, there is no legislation or any other guidelines that can control and comprehend the intentions of the human heart. For the heart, the basis of true motivation, has a profound influence and large control over the immeasurable neurons of the human brain. Reliable medical information shows that accident-prone persons display insubordinate traits whereby certain habits conducive to his knowledge, or lack of it, are usually deficient of emotional restraint, being either anxious and tense or easily angered and frustrated. These temperamental tendencies are instrumental with defects in judging the reflex ability of the body. Under certain circumstances and conditions, long established rules may be ignored, tending to feel subconsciously, one can handle any situation that arises. The unexpected now becomes the impossible. A familiar feeling to many in expressional terms, is, "It won't happen to me". So, we must conclude that individual personality is involved.

In view of the foregoing, we must remember at this stage in the journey, apart from the weather abnormallity, and being extremely late, everything else was seemingly normal. But because of the forced circumstances, Trew was understandably under stress, after all, he was not a remotely controlled robot, but a human. For this reason it is true to say that anxiety creates chemical reactions in the body cells, the metabolism that provides energy for normal brain function. Trew, being extremely cold at Cannon Street, and now with a low water supply, plus the fog restricting his way, were all contributory factors which may have instilled a mental "thorn in the flesh". According to information given, the lack of nutritive substance in the body results in mental pressure and anxiety, and has an unfavourable effect on the normal thinking processes and reflex control.

Visibility from Cannon Street to New Cross, according to provisional records, was about 70 to 100 yards; not too bad for picking out signals as they came into view. As mentioned in chapter three, this stretch of line is suspended on brick arches above the streets of South East London and continues for nearly four miles to New Cross, and because of the high elevation the fog was probably less dense than at ground level.

It is only a minute exaggeration in my view to conclude that Driver Trew knew every brick in the viaduct over which he was now progressing. His speed on passing the blue and white lights of Peak Freans biscuit factory, promulgating their centenary year, was sustained perhaps at 30mph. The speed under normal conditions was just over fifty to maintain the four minutes allowed to New Cross from London Bridge. For every precious minute that elapsed 20 seconds was lost, but no matter, time, under this persuasive environment must be disregarded.

Further on, each green light must have added a glow of optimism for Trew's perceptive powers, for everything so far favoured a clear run, well at least to Sevenoaks. Swaying majestically over Trundleys Road, the line at this juncture swings into a slow right curvature before straightening out to enter New Cross station. It also advocated an abrupt end to the brick arches. At ground level now, the train distinctively changed tune, from an abrasive hollow melody to a smooth and solid symphony, an overture not readily appreciated at the nearby New Cross Empire, (since demolished). My own experience when working trains over that same section was that the Ramsgate express may have increased its speed slightly before gliding smoothly through New Cross station.

Trew had no problem observing the green signal (A42) at the end of New Cross platform. Passing this green aspect and under New Cross Road bridge, the stratosphere suddenly converted. The visibility was now down to 5 to 10 yards; not at all surprising at ground level. To add to the diabolism were retaining brick walls black with age and engine soot. It epitomised a deep 'chasm' with several bridges supporting the steep cutting. The scene could well depict the 'dark abyss' in the biblical account. This deepish shrouded cavern continued for nearly one mile, culminating at St John's station. The stratus was as black as the coal Fireman Hoare was now placing around his fire, for he realised the telling climb to the North Downs was only seconds away. Black smoke from the chimney therefore, must have added an extra burden to visibility.

The passengers who were conscious to reality, may have heard the change of tune under the wheels, but were in no position to identify the change in visibility. Driver Trew, now driving blind, knew exactly where he was though, within a brick or two. His ears told him what his eyes could not. He knew there was a short sharp tunnel and two signals before St John's station. Sadly, it was at this stage in the journey that things went tragically wrong for Trew. His optimism did not accept cautionary signals, why should he?, after all, every aspect so far had been green he perhaps reasoned. Hence, his subconscious influence became positively convincing, he had never, in all his years as driver, had reason to stop between New Cross and St John's, so why must it be different this time? Also, he needed the current momentum, as slow as it was, to punch the train up the bank and on past Parks Bridge and on through Hither Green. Clearly, Driver Trew was ready to 'open' the regulator, rather than cut power to stop. Therefore, to stop the train must have been far from his mind, thus allowing the unexpected to become the impossible.

Unfortunately he did not spot the mute outer home signal (L16) exposing a cautionary 'two yellow' lights. I must point out also, that the fire-hole doors were fully open due to Fireman Hoare feeding the fire. The bright glare did not help the driver. On passing L16, the incandescent glow may have superficially obliterated the signal and blended as one. L16 and the following L17 signal were both positioned on the fireman's side. In normal circumstances both lights were easily observed by the driver, for the road from New Cross was a slow left curve, but, on this 'abnormal' occasion, with only 5 to 10 yards visibility, Trew had no chance whatsoever, of seeing the signals in question.

In my opinion thus far, there was only one possible explanation why driver Trew did not cross the footplate to satisfy himself of the next signal display. It would be reasonable to conclude, without condemnation, that the sudden fog density did not register quickly. Trew was expecting to see signals L16 and L17 from his own side, just as he had observed all other signals previously, but may I add, within at least 70 yards visibility. Therefore, it is seemingly obvious, that the unanticipated heavy density caught Driver Trew unawares.

In this dramatic account, signal L18, located at the end of St John's platform flagrantly embellished a 'red' light and was subsequently protecting the Hayes commuter already anchored (brakes hard on) on the succeeding red light. The rear of the ten car electric Hayes train was only 138 yards ahead of signal L18. A very small margin indeed.

On the approach to St John's station, Driver Trew requested his mate to look out for the next signal, not for one moment believing it could be red. Simultaneously the station lights came into view exposing the thick shroud. It was at this point that the driver must have realised he had passed L16 and L17 escaping their notice. For reasons already mentioned, Trew was not anticipating cautionary measures. Therefore, when the fireman saw the red glow of signal L18, he shouted an instant warning. But HORROR of HORRORS, Trew's brain refused to accept what he now heard. The unexpected became impossible. He was thus momentarily mesmerised. The regulator valve was still part open and, instead of immediately dropping the handle, (to apply complete brake pressure) he chose to shut the regulator first. In his brief confusion two valuable seconds were lost. When the brake was applied it was far too late, for the train's momentum and pushing weight careered unchecked and soon gobbled up the 138 yards margin before brake pressure took effect. The three or four seconds, from the time Hoare saw the red light, resulted in 'no' speed reduction. *Spitfire* smashed into the stationary (400 tons) Hayes train at about 30mph with appalling consequences. Thirty seven persons died in the Hayes train and 53 perished in the Ramsgate express. One hundred and nine were severely injured, which included the fireman. Driver Trew, although severely shocked and remorsed escaped with minor injury.

From the Lewisham end of St John's platform (now removed) to the point of the crash the track cambers and rises at 1 in 218. According to our mathematical experts, their calculations demonstrate that a 30mph train as heavy as the Ramsgate express can stop in a distance of 130 yards providing of course that maximum brake pressure is instantly enforced.

The rear of the engine tender and the front end of the leading carriage were pulverised together pitching into the central piers of a steel flyover. This girded flyover carried the Lewisham to Nunhead rail traffic over the Kent main line. Inevitably the bridge supports collapsed, bringing the 350 ton bridge on top of the three leading coaches of the Ramsgate train, crushing them like matchwood. Ironically, it was the St John's Ambulance Brigade who were the first on the scene.

Just two minutes after the devastations, Driver Corke was at the controls of an eight car electric train on the 'overhead' line from Nunhead unaware of what was before him. His slow approach was because of a red signal positioned the other side of the now collapsed flyover. Despite the hazardous condition, Driver Corke was able to see the flyover had twisted and subsided in front of him. Thankfully, because of the higher elevation, the fog was less dense, and as was usual on electric trains, the driver's observation windows are foremost. His prompt action stopped his packed train from certain disaster with literally 'no' seconds to spare. One's own imagination must represent what might have occurred had the Nunhead commuter been two minutes earlier. Gladly, that must remain pure speculation.

It is noteworthy to recall, from a non-critical point of view, certain extenuating events leading up to the disaster that fundamentally reveal how this horrific accident should have been prevented, and Driver Trew's error would have been between him and his whistle.

An oversight by the signalman at Parks Bridge Junction allowed two trains to stand behind each other at two separating sections that were protected by red signals respectively. Of course there is nothing unusual about that; the leading train was stopped at signal M10 on the 'down' main line, more or less opposite the Parks Bridge signal box. This however, was the 5.25 diesel electric Hastings train that was also behind schedule. Immediately behind the Hasting train, and stopped at signal M8 was the ill-fated Hayes commuter laden with up to 1,500 human sardines. (See diagram for train positions). I must point out also, that because of the disrupted schedules, the two stationary trains mentioned were in reverse order which, broadly speaking, favoured the Ramsgate driver. Sadly for Trew, signalman Beckett wrongly identified both trains in their correct sequence as per schedule. This was substantiated later regarding his own verbal report, that the Ramsgate train had hit the rear of the Hastings demu. How unfortunate for Trew that the signalman misunderstood the altered train sequence. With all respect to signalman Beckett, the Hastings diesel should *not* have been held at signal M10, for the main line was clear to Hither Green. Had Beckett known it was the Hastings train opposite his box, he would have no doubt but to allow it to proceed, and in so doing, the following Hayes train standing at M8 would have progressed to M10 and wait for road clearance before diverging right, (over the 'up' main line), and pick-up the Hayes route to Ladywell. Therefore, the section where the crash occurred would now remain completely free, extending a longer margin to accommodate Trew's error.

The other signalman at St John's correctly transmitted the information he received on his describing instrument that was also displayed at Parks Bridge box, showing the Hastings and Hayes train in that order. However, when a message is received by this relay method, the apparatus produces a distinct click and exhibits the message accordingly. Therefore, each signalman, on observing the display is then able to position the route required. The two trains in question were following at close quarters all the way from Charing Cross, and on passing St John's, the station signalman rightly transmitted two relays in quick succession. These (now primitive) instruments were only capable of displaying one description at a time, for the second message automatically cancels the first. Therefore, one can see quite clearly how signalman Beckett missed the first display, holding what he thought was the Hayes commuter at signal M10. How miserably unfortunate for Driver Trew.

Obviously though, if both stationary trains had pursued their normal sequence, the disaster could not have been prevented. As the Hayes train, that the signalman wrongly assumed, would have quite rightly been held at signal M10 to await clearance. The Hastings demu, stopped at M8 would have then received the full impact.

The Inspecting Officers who were investigating the cause of the crash, showed extreme sympathy and understanding during the trial. In due course Trew was charged with manslaughter in April 1958, but because of a dissent by the jury he was acquitted.

Driver Trew's misconception cost him dearly. The mental and traumatic agony he suffered, knowing he alone was responsible for the loss of 90 lives is far beyond expression. His anguish reflected a broken man.

Human fallibility, and the insubordinate impulses that inhibit involuntary reaction mean that all of us are subject to error, and nobody can claim absolution from that fact. Gravely, many pay a heavy price for their mistake, perhaps never fully comprehending the varied implications of why! Many others, on the other hand, simply 'get away' with it without serious repercussions. But for Driver Trew, we can only feel sorry, that through just one credulous mistake he fell victim to the unfathomable enigmas of false impression and misfortune, which undoubtedly stimulated his own untimely death.

9
A New Segment of Railway Technology

$\mathbf{F}$rom man's beginning he has measured events in a framework of time, though no man knows exactly what time is. It is reckoned to be among the most valuable things of which he is aware, for a segment of time that has passed can never be retrieved.

It is during the full course of one's experiences in life that a person is truly identified as the kind of person he is, perhaps even more so after his death, his name or reputation becomes something of greater value that often deserves recognition. This is certainly true of George Stephenson and many other mechanical engineers who subsequently followed in his footsteps. Their achievements paved the way to much greater and faster railway accomplishments.

Mr John Bright MP (1811-1889) had this to say concerning railways in his day, "Railways have rendered more service and have received less gratitude than any other institution in the land". For myself, those words still ring true to this day. Therefore, this chapter will show that, since 1968 in particular, the railways in Great Britain took on a completely new segment of modernisation, a streamlined era which deserves topmost gratitude for services rendered.

The roots of the new railway framework began, suprisingly, as far back as 1909 when electric traction was first introduced on the LBSCR. The first trains ran from Victoria to London Bridge via Denmark Hill in South East London. Although World War I dampened progress, it was right after the war that plans were approved to electrify all of South London suburbia. For starters, overhead cables were strung for the first stage of the project, but later, a third, conductor rail was favoured for reasons of simpler installation and for easier maintenance purposes. By the 1930s and thereafter electric trains became a familiar sight on both the LBSCR and the SECR. This was because both sections from 1923, were amalgamated into one company to form the new Southern Railway.

In due course, the cleaner and much faster services took up their commuter schedules to and from places such as Dartford, Orpington, Hayes, Addiscombe, Tattenham Corner, and regular services even went as far south as Brighton and Eastbourne on the Sussex coast.

Of course, electrification did not stop with the Southern. From

World War II and onwards, other railways were to follow suit. The new dimensions also included more improved signalling methods which were greatly enhanced by the colour light system, which inevitably knocked paint off the oblique semaphore type. Today, few main lines still offer the old semaphore arms and they are a fast-disappearing breed.

In more recent years we have seen the introduction of computerised signal boxes and other automated control systems that contribute richly to sustain greater reliability and safety to the railway network, the mainstay of railway operations.

Furthermore, continuous welded rails that sit on reinforced concrete sleepers, also permit trains to perform at well over 100 mph. With at least ten years already clocked, the HST (High Speed Train) diesel units will no doubt remain for a long time yet, so we can expect even greater things to come in this so-called 'Age of the Train'.

Interestingly, the present new technology has now been called the 'Microprocessor Revolution' which has had much effect, not only on the modernisation and efficiency of British Rail, but also on more and more people throughout the world.

It is indeed hard to believe, that these technological innovations were the stuff of science fiction as little as fifty years ago. Due to this new revolution, we now have digital clocks and watches, electronic calculators, video and telecommunication systems as well as many other benefits far too numerous to mention. All this has produced an overwhelming force which has quite definitely knocked the pressure out of steam forever, except for the hundreds of preservation societies which loyally lubricate the motions in a small, but nonetheless, significant way.

A little over 30 years ago, it was confidently announced that steam locomotives had an indefinite future in Britain. It was believed that they would maintain their grandeur well into the 21st century and, because of that belief, few people felt the need for preservation measures to be taken at that time. But how assuredly and dramatically the incursion came and how wrong steam philosophers proved to be! Although very sad, we have to say good-bye to a process which began in 1829 with Stephenson's *Rocket* and which ended officially in 1968, so quashing a segment of time never to be retrieved. Needless to say, 'Black Clouds and White Feathers' will no longer rule supremely over the English country gardens.